ALWAYS A WINNER

A Bible Commentary for Laymen/1 Samuel
BY CYRIL J. BARBER AND JOHN D. CARTER

G/L
REGAL
BOOKS™

A BIBLE
COMMENTARY
FOR LAYMEN

A Division of G/L Publications
Glendale, California, U.S.A.

Other good Regal reading in the Bible Commentary
for Laymen series:
  Where the Action Is (Gospel of Mark)
    by Ralph P. Martin
  Keep On Keeping On! (1 & 2 Thessalonians)
    by Harold L. Fickett, Jr.
  This Land Is Your Land (Joshua)
    by Paul E. Toms
  Loved and Forgiven (Colossians)
    by Lloyd John Ogilvie

Many of the Scripture quotations in this book are the
translations or paraphrases of the authors. Other
versions quoted from:
NASB, New American Standard Bible. © The Lockman
Foundation 1960, 1962, 1963, 1968, 1971. Used by
permission.
NIV, New International Version, New Testament. Copyright
© 1973 by New York Bible Society International. Used
by permission.
Phillips, THE NEW TESTAMENT IN MODERN ENGLISH, Revi
Edition, J.B. Phillips, Translator. © J.B. Phillips
1958, 1960, 1972. Used by permission of Macmillan
Publishing Co., Inc.

Second Printing, 1978

Published by
Regal Books Division, G/L Publications
Glendale, California 91209
Printed in U.S.A.

Library of Congress Catalog Card No. 77-72556
ISBN 0-8307-0497-3

CONTENTS

A Teaching Kit for use with *Always A
Winner* is available from your church
supplier.

FOREWORD

The historical books of the Old Testament are commonly regarded as spiritually profitless—unless they are indefensibly spiritualized. Though important to the scholar they have little value, it is often assumed, in helping people today understand themselves and their relationship to God. But in their illuminating discussion of Samuel, Saul and David, two Christians who are scholars in their own right show that the very opposite is true. These Old Testament books are remarkably rich in timeless insights which bear directly on the problems all of us struggle with in the late twentieth century. Instead of being irrelevant, Old Testament history, as interpreted by Drs. Barber and Carter, becomes a fascinating source of theological and psychological truth.

Vernon Grounds

PREFACE

Confusion characterizes our age. Intellectually, emotionally, and spiritually we are faced with almost total befuddlement. And frequently we feel that we are alone with our problems. The circumstances which surround us *seem* to verify the statement of the French philosopher, Jean-Paul Sartre, who wrote: "Man can count on no one but himself; he is alone, abandoned on earth in the midst of his infinite responsibilities, without help, with no other aim than the one he sets himself, with no other destiny than the one he forges for himself on this earth."

Those who accept Sartre's pessimistic view of life find that in and of themselves they are unequal to the difficulties which surround them.

It is significant, therefore, that in the Bible God has given us the answer to modern man's dilemma. The solution begins with a vital relationship with Himself (through His Son, Jesus Christ) and is furthered by the development of a strong internal God-consciousness. Equipped with this internal dynamic we can successfully handle the trials and injustices which we all encounter at one time or another.

But how is this achieved? In what specific way may we come to understand more of God's provision for us?

This book, centered in 1 Samuel, attempts to answer these questions. In the way Samuel was reared we have the opportunity to observe how a powerful internal dynamic may be instilled in children so that they may grow to adulthood with a strong commitment to spiritual principles. Then, as we follow the career of Samuel, we are able to learn from him how we, too, may triumph over life's inequities.

In the course of our inquiry we also consider the personality of Saul. As the Scriptures reveal more and more of the inner workings in his heart, we observe how his external orientation and the lack of submission to the will of God resulted in the kind of experience described by Jean-Paul Sartre. God had given Saul everything he needed to be successful. It was on account of his insensitivity and neglect of spiritual realities that he failed so ignominiously.

Finally, there is David, a shepherd, warrior and "outlaw," who was continuously harassed by his jealous father-in-law, Saul. In spite of the difficulties he faced and several failures (caused by lapses into an external orientation), he was able to maintain his emotional balance and rise above the circumstances which threatened to engulf him. The psalms he wrote during this period reveal his spiritual recovery and demonstrate his awareness of God's work in his life. In a very real sense the difficulties he faced and the spiritual victories he won were the means God used to prepare him for a life of effective service.

From the lives of these men—and the positive and negative examples they set—we see clearly the conflict between the flesh and the spirit which Paul described when he wrote: *Those who live according to their sinful nature have their minds set on what that nature desires; but those who*

8

live in accordance with the Spirit have their minds set on what the Spirit desires. The mind of sinful man is death, but the mind controlled by the Spirit is life and peace, because the sinful mind is hostile to God. It does not submit to God's law, nor can it do so. Those controlled by their sinful nature cannot please God. You, however, are controlled not by your sinful nature but by the Spirit, if the Spirit of God lives in you (Rom. 8:5-9, *NIV*). From these lessons we are shown how we too may be included in God's winners' circle.

The material in this book is designed for individual or group use. Each chapter has questions appended to it to aid in the internalization of its message. If the study of the Scriptures can be followed by discussion with a friend (or friends), then optimum results are sure to follow.

The authors wish to take this opportunity to thank those whose indefatigable efforts have made this book possible. Special thanks is also due Dr. Vernon C. Grounds, president of the Conservative Baptist Theological Seminary, Denver, Colorado, who, in the midst of a very busy schedule, took time out to read the manuscript and write the Foreword.

Cyril J. Barber
John D. Carter

1

TRAIN UP A CHILD

1 SAMUEL 1:1—3:21

In addressing a group of married couples at a weekend retreat, a renowned educator remarked, "The greatest misfortune that can befall a child is to have parents." He went on to explain that when parents are preoccupied with their own interests and neglect the mental and moral, emotional and spiritual development of their children, serious problems are bound to develop.

Examples of parental neglect are not hard to find. Quite recently, in New York City two 14-year-old boys and a 15-year-old girl staged a bank robbery. The police were secretly notified when the teller touched off an alarm button. The teenagers were soon apprehended. Later, at their arraignment in juvenile court, it was discovered that each child came from an upper-middle-class home.

When asked about the conduct of her son, one mother, a nominal Christian, replied, "Why would he do it? We've given him everything he ever wanted!"

A counselor appointed by the court later confirmed that the teenagers had indeed been given everything they asked for—everything except the loving attention of their parents. Their behavior was a plea for parental interest and companionship. The robbery had been preceded by a long series of misdemeanors, all committed with a view of obtaining attention. These young people were unconsciously acting out the old adage that "it is better to be beaten than to be ignored." The material gifts of their parents in no way compensated for the personal neglect they suffered. They had everything except a feeling of being wanted and appreciated for their own sake.

In another part of the country a mother brought her son to see their minister. His grades at school were barely passable. By way of contrast, his younger brother's academic record was good. "Why can't he be like his brother?" she complained.

It wasn't long before the pastor realized it was the mother who needed counseling. Constant criticism in the home, continuous comparison of her older son's performance at school with that of his younger brother (while ignoring his musical talent) had almost destroyed this young adolescent's sense of worth. He felt he was inferior, became introspective and lacked motivation.

Equally as tragic is the case of nine young people—five girls and four boys—ranging in age from 16 to 18 who were caught selling heroin on the campus of a midwestern high school. They all came from broken homes. Their mothers worked and over the years they had been left to fend for themselves. The monotony of the daily "grind" finally got to them. They felt unable to cope with their circumstances in a legitimate way. They started selling drugs "so that they could go out and do things."

In analyzing their situation, those responsible for determining what should be done with them came to the conclusion that the behavior of these teenagers was due to the lack

11

of any positive influence in their lives. To be sure, their mothers worked. However, if *quality* time had been spent with them, and constructive encouragement given them, they could have taken on some working responsibilities which would have made them feel that they were contributing to their homes and preparing for the future. The lack of parental involvement caused them to feel neglected. As a result, their lives lacked purpose and direction.

If these were isolated incidents, far removed from the mainstream of our lives, we might excuse ourselves by claiming that "our children are different." Unfortunately, recent studies indicate that parental neglect of children, even in Christian communities, is in large measure responsible for their deviant behavior. And even when the offense is not as overt as the ones already mentioned, Christian parents nevertheless find that the activities of their sons and daughters all too often reflect the attitude of their peer group rather than the influence of the home.

In the light of all this, how may Christian parents rear their children? What did Solomon have in mind when he said, *Train up a child in the way he should go, even when he is old he will not depart from it* (Prov. 22:6, *NASB*)?

Fortunately, the Bible illustrates for us both the precept for, as well as the practice of, rearing children (see Deut. 4:9,10; 6:7,20-25; 11:19; 32:7,46).

The Laboratory of Life

The *home* is to be the laboratory of life. It is the place where godliness is to be nourished and virtue encouraged. To those searching for guidance on how to rear their children, the example of Hannah and her husband, Elkanah, provides a real-life illustration of proper child development.

The training Hannah and Elkanah gave Samuel equipped him with an understanding of the world and his place in it. He felt loved, worthwhile and competent. He was also

12

given responsibility. These things contributed to his well-rounded development (see 1 Sam. 2:26).

Our image of Samuel has been created by an artist and perpetuated in a multitude of Sunday School papers. In our mind's eye we see him as a child kneeling in prayer while God speaks to him. Apart from this impression we know little of Samuel; and yet, as a result of the way in which he was reared, he was able to guide his people from a loose tribal confederation to a systematic and orderly form of government.

Samuel appears on the scene of biblical history after the Hebrews have been restored to the Promised Land. Following the death of Joshua, the nation was ruled by the judges. During this time the people continually did what was right in their own eyes (see Judg. 17:6; 21:25). In spite of God's goodness to them they turned from Him to worship the pagan gods of the nations about them. The Lord then allowed their enemies to oppress them. In their extremity they cried out to Him. He then raised up a judge who delivered them. During the lifetime of each judge a degree of material prosperity returned to the people. When the judge died, however, they would again apostatize and the cycle would repeat itself once more (see Judg. 2:11—3:6).

As we take up the story of Samuel we find that the most recent nation to begin oppressing the Israelites is the Philistines. They have superior weapons to those of the Hebrews and, with their chariots, control the lowlands to the south and the chief trade routes. They have also established garrisons at strategic locations in the hill country. Their presence brings the tribes in the middle and southern part of Canaan to the brink of economic ruin.

Dedication to God
1 Samuel 1:1-17

The home into which Samuel is born is a devout one.[1] Each year Elkanah goes to the house of the Lord in Shiloh and presents himself and his family before the Lord (see Exod. 23:16; 34:22).[2]

During these feasts, Elkanah's second wife,[3] Peninnah, would taunt Hannah because she had no children.[4] It is significant that the Bible uses the term "rival" to describe their relationship.

Hannah appears calm even under Peninnah's provocation. However, at the meal commemorating God's blessing to the family during the year, she refuses to eat. Elkanah at once notices this and attempts to console her by assuring her of his love. Another person might still have allowed her emotional frustration to override her reason. Not Hannah! She feels keenly Peninnah's rebuffs and is disappointed that God has withheld children from her; still, she does not act irresponsibly.

Rising superior to Peninnah's attempts to frustrate her because of her situation, a situation she is powerless to change, she shows her maturity by joining her husband, Peninnah and the rest of the family in the Feast.

Nothing, however, can compensate Hannah for the desired joy of motherhood. Inwardly, there is unrest. She longs for peace to replace the vexation brought on by Peninnah's callous reminder of her condition. And in this state of anxiety she seeks the Lord's presence.

We have no idea how long Hannah remained before the Lord. We do know that she prayed silently. This in itself is surprising for, in Israel, prayer and weeping before God, or other displays of strong emotion, have traditionally been most demonstrative. We also know that Hannah concluded her prayer with a vow: *If you will indeed look on the affliction of your maidservant and remember me [and] will give me a son, then I will give him to the LORD all the days of his life, and a razor shall never come on his head*[5] (1:11).

Hannah's vow would, of course, have to be ratified by Elkanah (see Num. 30:6-15). It would also have a far-reaching effect upon her child and his future. Her son would be separated from his fellows, easily identifiable by his long hair, and dedicated to lifelong service of the Lord.

Eli, the priest, is quick to observe Hannah as she prays. His assumption that she is drunk provides us with an unsolicited commentary on his own spiritual insensitivity and the moral conditions of the day (see 1 Sam. 1:13,14,16; compare 2:12,22-25). Hannah, however, replies to his unwarranted censure with dignity and calmness. Once again we see the maturity of her well-balanced personality. Then, without going into specifics, she says: *I am a woman oppressed in spirit . . . out of my great concern and provocation I have poured out my soul before the LORD* (1:15).

To this discreet reply Eli adds his blessing.

Faith to Meet the Challenge
1 Samuel 1:18-23

Hannah returns to the others. *And her face is no longer sad.* This is the Bible's way of saying that her faith had risen to meet the challenge and she believes God has heard her prayer.

Faith has three levels. There is the *acceptance* level at which a person merely acknowledges the validity of the truth presented. This involves the mental acceptance of certain facts without any life-changing decision on the part of the individual.

The second level deals with one's *preference.* At this level motivation can clearly be seen as the person acts upon his knowledge of truth. This is the level at which conversion takes place.

The third level is one of *commitment.* It involves complete identification. It was at this level that Hannah's faith operated! She committed her all to the Lord and trusted implicitly in His willingness to grant her request. And God honored her faith. In the course of time she conceived and, shortly before the next annual feast, Samuel was born. Elkanah and the rest of the family went to Shiloh as usual, but

Hannah remained in Ramah. She had apparently determined that the first time Samuel was presented at the temple he would remain there *in the service of God forever* (1:22).

Valued as a Person
1 Samuel 1:24—2:11

During the time Hannah nurses Samuel she has no other children (see 1 Sam. 2:19-21). She and her husband are able to spend time with Samuel and he becomes aware of the fact that he is wanted—he has value as a person. As his parents impart to him something of their own personalities, they impress on his child-mind his dedication to the Lord. This makes him feel special. It also gives him a sense of mission.

Every young child craves and deserves to receive these three ingredients: (1) a sense of *belonging* (or being loved), (2) the loving involvement of one's parents which creates a sense of *worth*, and (3) a sense of *purpose*. When these are lacking the door is opened to all sorts of problems. Even in homes where there is more than one child, and perhaps the mother works, parents can nevertheless instill into each child the realization that he is loved and appreciated. The *quality* of the time spent with each one can more than make up for whatever may be missing in quantity. A sense of direction can also be given children by early dedicating them to the Lord, and by letting them know that He has a special plan for their lives.

In rearing our children it is well for us to keep in mind the fact that nothing can take the place of our example. The personal dedication of Hannah and Elkanah may be seen from the way in which they fulfill their vow. Provision had been made in the law for the redemption of the firstborn (see Exod. 34:20; Num. 18:15). Neither Hannah nor Elkanah avail themselves of this provision. To Hannah, the highest calling of which she can conceive involves giving

16

her dearest possession to the Lord. As soon as Samuel has been weaned she takes him to Shiloh.[6] In presenting him before Eli, she says: *For this boy I prayed; and the LORD has given me my petition which I asked of Him. Therefore I have lent him to the LORD: as long as lives he is lent to the LORD* (1:27,28).

With such an example before him, an example which required Elkanah's concurrence, it is no wonder that Samuel bows and *worships the LORD there.* He does not yet know God from personal experience (see 1 Sam. 3:7), but his heart is already inclined in the right direction. He gladly accepts the role he is to play and willingly submits himself to the One who means so much to his parents.

As Samuel begins to assist Eli in the work of the temple, a further ingredient is added to the development of his personality. He is given *responsibility.* We can be sure that a child with Samuel's sense of purpose (or mission) would diligently discharge his duties. And with the completion of each task, there would come the feeling of accomplishment and a growing sense of competence.

Elements of Training
1 Samuel 2:12—3:21

We make a grave mistake if we conclude that from the time Samuel is left at Shiloh he is bereft of all maternal concern.[7] There are women there, around the temple, who perform regular duties in connection with the sanctuary.[8] They gladly *attend to the bodily needs and domestic training* of the young child. Furthermore, confirmation of the fact that he has not been abandoned is provided yearly when his family visits Shiloh. Each year his mother brings him a new tunic, and as they spend time together Samuel realizes afresh how much he means to his parents.[9]

Neither is Samuel's moral and spiritual training neglected. As William J. Deane has pointed out in his book on *Samuel and Saul: Their Lives and Times,*[10] Eli must have *taught Samuel the Law and the history of his people.* Deane is also of the opinion that "the old priest took better care of him [Samuel] than he had of his own sons, and attended more scrupulously to his training." This was the *positive* instruction Samuel received.

The *negative* instruction takes the form of the *evil example of Eli's sons* (see 1 Sam. 2:12-17,22-26). They are the theological liberals of their day. They despise the holy, hold in contempt God's prescribed method whereby the priests participate in the sacrificial meal, chafe under the restraints of the Law (see Deut. 12:12; Lev. 7), and copy the licentious practices of the pagan nations around them.[11] They know no law but the law of their carnal appetites; and from their evil practices Samuel turns away.

Another form of Samuel's education is *direct communication from the Lord.* One night he hears someone call his name. In obedience he runs to Eli. Eli, however, states he has not called him and tells Samuel to go back to bed. Three times this happens.

Finally Eli perceives that it must be the Lord. He tells Samuel what to do, and in the morning inquires of the message God has given him. The story, as well as Samuel's reply, is well known. God tells Eli through Samuel that He has marked out the old priest's sons for judgment (3:11-14). The significance of this revelation, however, does not lie in what will happen to Eli and his house, but in the fact that it openly attests Samuel as *the prophet of the LORD.* From now on Eli is to be set aside. Previously, word from the Lord had been rare; visions were infrequent. Now God begins to work through Samuel, and *he lets none of His words fall to the ground. And all Israel ... knows that Samuel is confirmed a prophet of the LORD* (3:19,20).

The Importance of Influence

In evaluating all that took place in the life of Samuel, it is of value for us to notice that Samuel enjoyed proper development (2:26). He grew physically and spiritually, mentally and emotionally. The jealous rivalry in his home in Ramah did not distort his personality, neither did the sensual and irreligious example of Eli's sons warp his moral values. His entire life was given meaning and direction by his parents. From an early age he was given responsibility in the temple. This helped him develop confidence. From these experiences Samuel came to understand the world and his place in it. He developed a strong internal God-consciousness and was prepared for a lifetime of service.

These ingredients are the very things that are missing in so many homes today. They can easily be supplied by showing our children they are wanted, by spending time with them, by providing them with a sense of mission and by giving them responsibility. Equipped with this preparation they will be ready to face the future with the confidence of a winner. In the rearing of children, the home (not the church or the school) is central. There is no synthetic replacement for a decent home life. Our high crime rate, particularly among juveniles, is directly traceable to a breakdown in moral fiber—to the disintegration of home and family life. Religion and home life are complementary. Each strengthens the other. It is seldom that a solid and wholesome home life can be found in the absence of religious inspiration.

Several years ago Ruth Graham, wife of evangelist Billy Graham, came to Dr. V. Raymond Edman, who was then President of Wheaton College. "Prexy," she asked, "if you had it to do over again, what would you do differently for your children?" To this earnest inquiry Dr. Edman replied, "There are many things I would do differently. Especially, I would deliberately, even doggedly, take more time to be with my children . . . If I had it to do over again, we would have more time for reading and playing together, for picnics and trips. Reading, playing and praying together add love and security to young hearts."

Hannah's time with Samuel was limited. Her example proves that our loving involvement with our children is of the greatest importance in shaping young lives and preparing them for the future. Our next chapter will show how spiritual renewal may be maintained and what happens when our ways please the Lord.

Interaction

1. Why doesn't God always answer our prayers? (See Matt. 21:21,22; John 15:7, etc.) Are there times when your life, when your experience differs from what the Bible appears to teach? Is this how Hannah may have felt in light of promises from God to her? (See Deut. 7:14.) What may we learn from the way in which Hannah prayed in terms of: (1) our *submission* to the will of God (see Matt. 26:39,42—compare Hannah's use of the word "maidservant" in 1 Sam. 1:11); (2) our *identification* with the purpose of God (praying in Christ's name, John 14:13,14 —compare Hannah's use of the term Lord as explained in footnote 2); (3) our *fervency* in claiming the promise of God (see Jas. 5:17,18—compare Hannah's "pouring out her soul" in 1 Sam. 1:15); (4) our *faith* in the provision of God (see 1 John 5:14,15—compare Deut. 7:14). Are all these characteristics necessary for prayer to be effective?

2. Explore the ways in which your children may be given a deeper sense of being wanted; a realization of your love for them; and a sense of purpose and direction in life. Which of these do you have greatest difficulty providing? How may this be remedied?

3. Samuel's home was one of bickering and strife. In what ways was he able to rise above the jealousies and tensions created by Peninnah and her children?

4. Children and young people learn from both positive and negative situations. Do you think Christian parents are inclined to be overprotective? Why? How may social evils be offset by training in the home? What can you do to prepare your children for the realities of life?

20

5. What do we learn of Samuel's early development through his interaction with Eli in 1 Samuel 3:15-18?

Footnotes

1. All male Israelites were supposed to appear before the Lord three times each year (see Exod. 23:14-17). This rule, however, "had never been observed, and certainly in the unsettled times which succeeded the death of Joshua had fallen into desuetude [so that] one public attendance in the year was thought sufficient even by religious and scrupulous people." See "Festivals" in *Unger's Bible Dictionary* (Chicago: Moody, 1961), pp. 350-363. It should be remembered that very little of God's Word had been written and that the people were entirely dependent upon the priests for their religious knowledge. If the priesthood was decadent, so were the people.

2. The use of the term LORD (for the Hebrew *Yahweh*) is most significant. *Yahweh* (sometimes rendered Jehovah) is the name used of God to indicate His unique covenant relationship with Israel. Elkanah was mindful of this and lived under the conditions of the covenant.

3. Polygamy was not uncommon in Old Testament times. It was frequently resorted to in order to insure that a man would have a son to carry on his name and perpetuate his inheritance (see Num. 27:9-11). It also ensured that the women of his household would be cared for in the event of his death. See Roland de Vaux, *Ancient Israel* (New York: McGraw-Hill, 1961), pp. 53-55.

4. To go childless in Near Eastern cultures was regarded as a mark of divine judgment. Those who were unable to bear children not only bore a social stigma, but faced grounds for divorce. On account of her barrenness, Hannah no doubt forfeited some of her status as Elkanah's principal wife. She also suffered from lowered self-esteem and had to endure the reproach of her peers.

5. The son for whom Hannah prayed would be dedicated to the Lord, not as a Levite whose duties commenced when he was 25 and continued until he was 50 (see Num. 4:3; 8:24,25), but as a *perpetual* Nazarite (see Num. 6:2-21).

6. Children in Near Eastern lands were normally weaned at three years of age. See Roland de Vaux, *Ancient Israel*, pp. 42,43; and evidence from the non-canonical book of Second Maccabees 7:27.

7. Dorothy Zeligs, in *Psychoanalysis and the Bible* (New York: Bloch, 1974), believes that Samuel's separation from his parents could only have been construed by the young child as "abandonment," with the usual shattering effects to his emotional development. This need not have been the case, and certainly Hannah would have guarded against such a traumatic reaction. Her preparation of Samuel for his life's work, and the way she instilled in him the privilege of being set apart to the Lord, would have

21

minimized the agony of parting and the usual sense of loss. (Zeligs writes from a strongly Freudian, anti-supernaturalistic perspective.)

8. Several passages of Scripture bear on this theme, among them Exodus 38:8 and Psalm 68:11. It is probable that Anna the prophetess was one of them (see Luke 2:36-38). These women were not always the most virtuous (see 1 Sam. 2:22; 2 Kings 23:7), but some of their number would certainly have made suitable foster-mothers for young Samuel.

9. The fact that Samuel was denied the close ties of home had a two-fold effect upon him. He grew to manhood with a vibrant internal (spiritual) orientation. He had a strong sense of God's will for his life. He also tended to be isolated socially and this may be traceable to his dedication to be a Nazarite as well as the fact that his contact with youths of his own age was minimal. This may, in turn, have affected his relationship with his sons. It should be remembered that a Nazarite vow was *normally* for a limited period of time, not for life; and that playmates and friends are an integral part of proper development. In these particulars Samuel's service at the temple from the age of three years constituted an exception rather than the rule.

10. W.J. Deane, *Samuel and Saul: Their Lives and Times* (London: James Nisbet, Pub., n.d.), p. 19.

11. When the Bible speaks of Israel "playing the harlot" on every high hill and under every green tree, more than spiritual apostasy from the Lord is in view (see Jer. 2:20; 3:1,2,6; Ezek. 16:15,16,28,29; see also Deut. 12:2,3; 1 Kings 14:22-24; 2 Kings 16:3,4; 17:8-12; 2 Chron. 21:11, etc.). The sensual worship begun by Nimrod's wife, Semiramis, ultimately centered in the fertility cult and dominated the religious beliefs and practices of the Near East. Cult prostitution became popular, and those in Israel who were of a more liberal persuasion preferred these fleshly practices to the austere, self-denying worship prescribed by Moses.

2
OUR CONVULSIVE ERA
1 SAMUEL 4:1—7:17

For several decades church historians have claimed that we are living in the post-Christian era of American history. The high hopes of our founding fathers for a Christian society seem to have run aground on the rocky reef of encroaching secularism. The result has been widespread disillusionment among both clergy and laity.

In his book, *A Christian America: Protestant Hopes and Historical Realities*, Robert T. Handy[1] describes the aim of the men who founded our nation. In tracing our history Dr. Handy shows that when the ideal of our fathers for a Christian society failed, hope for the progress of Christianity was not abandoned; the era of the revivalists was born. Unfortunately, the expectations of these evangelists were likewise unsuccessful. To be sure, many thousands of people were converted but the work of these men did not make any

23

lasting impact upon society. In time, the historic roots of the revival movement were forgotten and people adjusted to regular evangelistic meetings. Today the emphasis has shifted to church renewal. But whereas people formerly knew what they wanted, disillusionment over the past has caused confusion in the present. The search now is for something reliable on which we may hang our hopes; we do not want to face disappointment again. Failure, however, seems inevitable if for no other reason than a lack of agreement on the part of our religious leaders as to what is involved in "renewal."

In 1 Samuel 7, God has seen fit to outline the basic fundamentals of genuine spiritual renewal. As we study this chapter we shall find that we can learn important principles of renewal from these ancient Israelites.

The chapter may be divided as follows: (1) the historic setting, verses 1,2; (2) the challenge to reform, verses 3,4; (3) the convocation at Mizpah, verses 5-11; (4) the commemoration of victory, verses 12-14; and (5) the continuity of Samuel's ministry, verses 15-17.

However, before concentrating our attention on the principles of renewal in chapter 7 we need to consider the events which led up to the spiritual restoration of the people. To do so we must go back to chapter 4.

The Interval Between
1 Samuel 4:1—7:2

In chapter 4 we find that the Philistines had again invaded the land. They were formidable fighters led by a military aristocracy. With their superior weapons and skill they constituted the kind of threat with which the Hebrews could not cope.[2]

A decisive blow was struck by the Philistines near Aphek. After the first encounter the Israelites decided that they needed help. Having a strong religious heritage their thoughts naturally turned God-ward. His presence with

24

them was symbolized by the Ark of the Covenant. The Ark played an important part in their history in the past, why not now? Feeling that, with the Ark in their midst, they would be invincible they sent to Shiloh and brought the Ark into their camp (4:3-8).[3]

Instead of the expected victory, they met with humiliating defeat (4:10,11). The Philistines captured the Ark and proceeded to occupy the land. The sanctuary at Shiloh was destroyed and the people were deprived of any outward form of unity. To prevent the manufacture of any weapons and protect their own monopoly, the Philistines forced the Israelites to shut down their metal industry (see 1 Sam. 13:19-22). The old cycle of the book of Judges was repeating itself once more.

But what of Samuel? In the face of all these calamities, what happened to him? Where did he go after Shiloh was destroyed? How did he spend the 20 years which elapsed between chapters 4 and 7?

Many Bible scholars believe that "the schools of the prophets" came into being during this period.[4] From 1 Samuel 7:16 we know that Samuel went on an annual preaching mission to Bethel, Gilgal and Mizpah before returning to his home in Ramah. It is significant that the Bible mentions prophetic institutions in Bethel (see 2 Kings 2:3), Gilgal (see 2 Kings 4:38), Ramah (see 1 Sam. 19:19,20), and elsewhere (see 2 Kings 6:1). The constitution and object of these schools was comparable to the theological colleges of our day. Into these schools were gathered promising students and here they were trained for the office they were afterwards destined to fill. In all probability they received some of their training directly from Samuel. And as they put into practice the truths they were taught, they carried the message Samuel presented to them into the towns and villages of Israel.

In addition, during the 20 years the Ark was in Kiriath-Jearim, Samuel engaged in a persistent preaching mission of his own (see 1 Sam. 3:19—4:1; 7:6,17). This ministry finally bore fruit when some of the Israelites *began to lament after the LORD* (7:2). At last they realized that their spiritual corruption had caused their economic ruin (see Jer. 7:12). The stage was now set for their spiritual renewal.

The Search Within
1 Samuel 7:3-17

As we turn to chapter 7 we find that Samuel has his finger on the pulse of the people.

A challenge to reform. Samuel sees the early signs of their willingness to repent and issues them a challenge to reform (7:3,4). In doing so he reminds them of their unique relationship with their covenant-keeping God. *If you return to the LORD with all your heart, remove the foreign gods [Baal, god of the storm and king of the Canaanite pantheon] and the Ashtaroth [the goddess of fertility and war],*[5] *and direct your hearts to the LORD and serve Him alone; then He will deliver you from the hand of the Philistines.*

Samuel's message is simple and direct. "Repent of your past attitude toward the Lord," he exhorts. "Renounce the things which are hindering your spiritual life and rededicate yourselves to His service. Then, on the basis of His covenant relationship with you, God will deliver you!"

As a sign of their earnestness, the Israelites follow Samuel's command. To renounce their idolatry was a greater sacrifice than we at first suppose. As Dr. W.G. Blaikie points out, "To put away Baalim and Ashtaroth was to abjure what was fashionable and agreeable." It was to turn aside from the sensual religious practices of the pagans "and fall back on what was unattractive and sombre."[6]

A convocation at Mizpah. Assured of the sincerity of the people, Samuel summons them to a convocation at Mizpah (7:5-11). There on the high plateau the people congregate and, drawing water, pour it out before the Lord. Inasmuch as water, once poured on the ground, cannot be gathered up again, the people seem to be indicating the irrevocability of their decision to follow God's will.[7] It is as if they are giving themselves to the Lord with no thought of ever going back on their decision.

Fasting [8] and confession accompany the pouring of water on the ground. *And Samuel judges the sons of Israel there* (7:6). He acts on behalf of the Lord for those who are unsure of their standing before God (because of some specific sin in their lives) or are ignorant of what He requires of them.

It is during this convocation that the Philistines choose to attack the defenseless Israelites. They may have felt that the Hebrews were planning to rebel against them. If so, then a confrontation on Israelite soil was preferable to an invasion of their own land. In any event, this unprovoked attack is not what the Hebrews were expecting. They only recently renewed their allegiance to the Lord and might well question, "Is this the way our repentance is to be rewarded?" Such occurrences, however, are not uncommon. Whenever anyone begins to put things right with God, unexpected difficulties arise to test the reality of their dedication.

The fear of the Israelites is expressed in verse 8. Knowing from experience how merciless the Philistines are they entreat Samuel to pray for them. While the Philistines are scaling the heights of Mizpah, Samuel offers a suckling lamb as a whole burnt offering. This specific sacrifice symbolizes the entire consecration of the people to the Lord. Samuel then intercedes for them. God's response is immediate (see Isa. 65:24).

He thunders [9] with a great thunder . . . against the Philistines and smites them [apparently with hail], so that they are routed before Israel. And the men of Israel go out of Mizpah and pursue the Philistines, and strike them down . . . so the Philistines are subdued and they do not come any

27

more within the border of Israel all the days of Samuel (7:10-13).

Whereas formerly the Philistines had been God's instru-ment to chasten Israel, now that the people have been restored to His favor, the enemies of Israel immediately become the enemies of the Lord. The benefits of repentance are immediate. The defeat of the Philistines is very thorough. So thorough, in fact, that they make no attempt to rally after the storm has passed. They are afraid to enter into the territory of the Hebrews all the days of Samuel.[10] Furthermore, the border cities which formerly belonged to the Israelites are now restored to them.

The commemoration of victory. In commemorating this victory (7:12-14), Samuel erects an appropriate memorial (7:12). The location chosen for the pillar is the site of the Philistine debacle. Ironically, it is also the place of Israel's ignominious defeat 20 years earlier when thousands of Israelites were slain (see 1 Sam. 4:1,2,10,11). And Samuel calls the place *Ebenezer,* saying, *Thus far the LORD has helped us.*

It is fitting that the beginning of God's mercies should be acknowledged with thanksgiving. All too often in the joy of His deliverance His people forget to praise Him for His goodness to them.

A further result of Israel's new standing before the Lord is that there is now peace between them and the Amorites (see Prov. 16:7). These southern neighbors are afraid to continue their harassment of Israel now that God has once again shown Himself strong on their behalf (see Deut. 2: 25). The benefits of this victory are due, in large measure, to the influence of one man—Samuel (7:13). To be sure, the conquest of the Philistines was given them by the Lord.

The continuity of ministry. However, it was the persistent continuity of Samuel's ministry (7:15-17) during 20 long years of oppression and his continued influence over the people after the events at Mizpah that kept their enemies at bay. His life proves again that wherever the character of a godly man is such as to recall God, there the idea of a supernatural power is conveyed, and a certain over-awing influence is felt.

The Secret of Renewal

But what does all this have to do with you and me? Why should we be concerned with these ancient Israelites when our society has renounced the principles upon which our founding fathers established this nation?

The story of Samuel gives us hope in the midst of spiritual decline. Many are becoming discouraged because of the encroaching worldliness. Men are leaving the ministry and going into secular business because they have failed to see any lasting "fruit" from their labors.

Draw strength from the Lord. What we need today are men who, as with Samuel, will draw strength from their relationship with the Lord (1 Sam. 7:13) and persevere in teaching their congregations *the whole counsel of God* (Acts 20:27). In addition, the church needs men and women who are prepared to exercise the gifts the Holy Spirit has given them and tenaciously engage in the work of the Lord (see Heb. 6:10-12). This will encourage pastors and further the ministry of the local church.

Renew allegiance to the Scriptures. Furthermore, if there are to be any lasting results there must be renewed allegiance to the Scriptures as the inspired revelation of God to man. God's Word was never intended to be a book for scholars and specialists. From the very beginning it was intended to be everybody's book. Unfortunately, few take the time to become familiar with its contents. Being ignorant of God's will they are unable to walk acceptably before Him. The result is a society which bears a marked resemblance to the one of Samuel's day.

Recommit your life to God. Following Samuel's persistent ministry, the people *lamented after the LORD* (1 Sam.

29

7:2,4). They began to realize that sin had robbed them of God's blessing. Samuel sensed that the time was right for a recommitment of their lives to the One whom they professed to serve. He therefore summoned them to meet at Mizpah. The people obeyed Samuel's summons, showed true repentance by renouncing their idolatrous practices and dedicated themselves unreservedly to the Lord.

Repentance—turning from sin to God—and *confession* seeing our failures and wrongdoing from God's standpoint, always precedes spiritual renewal. "Some things," as Epictetus has observed, "are confessed with ease, but others with difficulty." Israel's renunciation of the sensual religious practices of the pagan nations and recommittal of themselves to the God of their fathers lay at the very heart of His subsequent intervention on their behalf (see Deut. 4:29-31; 2 Chron. 7:14; Joel 2:12,13).

The problem with us is that frequently our repentance does not last very long. So often we turn from those things which we know are displeasing to the Lord when we are in trouble, only to revert back to them when the difficulty is past. When this happens, our repentance resembles a temporary change of opinion rather than a permanent change of heart. This is why we need to renounce the things that have wooed us away from the Lord (see 2 Cor. 4:2). A truly repentant person thinks God's thoughts about sin, takes God's side against self, and turns to Him in humility and contrition (see Ps. 34:18,19; 51:17; Isa. 57:15).

Remain dependent on God. In much the same way that the Israelites were faced with an immediate threat by their former masters (1 Sam. 7:7,8), so the repentant Christian is at once tempted by the very sin (secret or overt) which has so long held him in subjection. He must remain wholly dependent upon God.

Augustine experienced this kind of situation soon after his conversion. He tells us about it in his *Confessions*. One day while walking down the street he saw his former mistress. She also saw him. Augustine turned and began to walk away, but the woman with whom he had lived for so many years tried to catch up with him. "Augustine," she called, "it is I."

To this Augustine replied as he broke into a run, "Yes, but it is not I." He was a new man in Christ (see 2 Cor. 5:17) and reckoned himself dead to the things which had characterized his former manner of life (see Rom. 6:1-14).

The essence of Christianity is that God is able to give us *victory in the place of our former defeat.* This should not only be over the "gross" sins, but over the secret transgressions of the heart as well. Our experience should be similar to the apostle Paul's, who could say that his life was a continuous pageant of triumph in Christ (see 2 Cor. 2:14-16; 4:1,2).

Extend your scope of influence. As Samuel's influence over the nation increased (1 Sam. 7:15-17), even so the person who experiences this kind of renewal will enjoy ever-widening circles of influence.

As Pascal pointed out, "The serene beauty of a holy life is the most powerful influence in the world next to the power of God." The extent of his power will be in direct proportion to his conformity to the will of God. Those who submit to His will will be amazed at what God can accomplish through them.

This is true spiritual renewal! It prepares us for a life of significant service and, as we shall see, helps us face adversity with equanimity.

Interaction

1. How would you define idolatry? What is its twentieth-century counterpart (see 1 Sam. 15:23; Col. 3:5; etc.)? Why is it hard for us to put away the "idols" of self-will or covetousness? What remedy has God provided for us (see Rom. 6:1-11; 12:1-8; Col. 3:1-17)?
2. From the history of the Israelites, what would you say is the

31

root cause of spiritual apathy? What were its results? How does the experience of the Israelites parallel ours today?

3. What place should *repentance* and *confession* have in the life of the believer? Why? What Scriptures support this view?

4. In Eli's time there was a *famine of hearing the words of the LORD* (1 Sam. 3:1). What caused this spiritual famine? How did Samuel meet the need? What application does this have for us?

5. God prospered Israel because of the influence of one man. In what specific ways may the Holy Spirit's control (see Eph. 5:18) of your life increase the area of your influence?

Footnotes

1. Robert T. Handy, *A Christian America: Protestant Hopes and Historical Realities* (New York: Oxford University Press, 1971).

2. For an evaluation of Philistine weapons and strategy see Yigael Yadin's *The Art of Warfare in Bible Lands* (New York: McGraw-Hill, 1963), II: 248-253,336-345,354f. A general discussion of the place and importance of the Philistines in Old Testament history may be found in Edward E. Hindson's *The Philistines and the Old Testament* (Grand Rapids: Baker, 1971).

3. The Israelites regarded the Ark as a "talisman," or good luck charm. They treated it as people today would a rabbit's foot. With it they felt assured of success. They made the mistake of placing their confidence in an object (the Ark of the Covenant) instead of a Person (the God of the Covenant). They were of the same company as those who substitute things (i.e., church membership or the sacraments) for a vital relationship with God through Jesus Christ.

4. William Foxwell Albright in his Goldenson Lecture, "Samuel and the Beginnings of the Prophetic Movement in Israel," Hebrew Union College, 1961; also in his book *Yahweh and the God's of Canaan* (Garden City, N.Y.: Doubleday, 1968), pp. 208-213.

5. This goddess appears with different names (e.g., Asherah, Astarte, Anat, etc.). The best discussion available is J.B. Pritchard's *Palestinian Figurines in Relation to Certain Goddesses Known Through Literature* (Philadelphia: University of Pennsylvania Press, 1943). Several other important works are also worthy of serious consideration. These include Arvid S. Kapelrud's *The Violent Goddess* (Oslo, Norway: Universitets-forlaget, 1969); U. Casutto's *The Goddess Anath* (Jerusalem: Magnes, 1971); John Gray's *The Legacy of Canaan* (Leiden, the Netherlands: E.J. Brill, 1965); E.O. James' *The Cult of the Mother-Goddess* (London: Thames and Hudson, 1959); S.N. Kramer's

The Sacred Marriage Rite (Bloomington, IN: Indiana University Press, 1969); and Raphael Patai's, *The Hebrew Goddess* (New York: Ktav, 1965).

6. W.G. Blaikie, *The First Book of Samuel*, the Expositor's Bible (Grand Rapids: Eerdmans, 1956), vol. 2, p. 27.

7. A similar expression is found in Lamentations 2:19. Alfred Edersheim in *Bible History of the Old Testament* (Grand Rapids: Eerdmans, 1954), vol. 4, p. 25f. presents a variety of views interpreting this incident.

8. In its biblical context, fasting involves being so given up to God (in confession, intercession or worship) that the individual becomes oblivious to the passing of time. God never intended that by denying the flesh we are then able to force Him to answer our prayers.

9. The first-century Jewish historian, Josephus, in his *Antiquities of the Jews*, VI:2:2, states that the thunder was accompanied by an earthquake. He also claims that many of the Philistines fell into the cracks that appeared in the earth. This is pure conjecture and there is no evidence for such a theory.

10. Later on we find that the Philistines have established garrisons in the land (see 1 Sam. 9:16; 10:5), and the Ammonites are threatening their borders (see 1 Sam. 11:1; 12:12). This appears to be in conflict with 1 Samuel 7:13. It seems likely that as long as Israel followed Samuel, their enemies were kept at bay. When he grew old their commitment to the Lord began to wane. Their enemies then began to encroach on their territory, and this brought—not a return to the Lord—but a demand for a king.

TOMORROW'S YESTERDAY

1 SAMUEL 8:1-22

There are many causes of emotional hurt. Rejection is one of them. The pain of rejection is very personal, for it attacks our feeling of worth. It is also very persistent, and if it is not handled properly, it will have far-reaching effects on our lives.

The pain of rejection results from a denial of *approval*, *affection* or *recognition* by an emotionally significant person or group. If we are unable to adequately cope with it, it will undermine our self-esteem, corrode our self-confidence, and give rise to feelings of insecurity, helplessness and frustration.

We are all familiar with the reaction of a child when he is reprimanded by his father. His father's *approval* means a great deal to him. He is deeply hurt by the reprimand and feels that he has been rejected. It is hard for him to live with this denial of approval.

The way in which the child expresses his feelings of

rejection comes from a basic need for security. His father's disapproval causes him to feel insecure. He therefore asserts himself against some other person (such as a younger brother or sister) or thing (like kicking a chair). He equates his assertiveness with strength and this exhibition of strength is designed to give him a feeling of security. Unfortunately, the demonstration of his hurt feelings may lead to further reproof and increased feelings of rejection. As he grows older he may learn not to show his resentment in such an obvious manner, but in repressing his feelings he will more than likely be laying the foundation for an overly-sensitive, bitter, hypercritical disposition.

Another form of rejection comes from denial of *affection*. It is common in the teenage years, but occurs at other times as well. One morning a woman dropped in to see her friend. It was really too early for "a social call." Her friend, however, sensed that something was wrong. As the story unfolded she found that her neighbor's husband had walked out on her. Their marriage had not been a happy one. Apparently that morning he had told her that he was tired of her constant criticism. He felt that nothing he did ever satisfied her.

In leaving his wife the husband was, in reality, showing his resentment for having been rejected (i.e., denied her affection). Now it was her turn to feel rejected.

And denial of *recognition* is equally hard to take. In recent months a national magazine has carried an article on the plight of some people who have been laid off their jobs. In their case, they had served their company faithfully for many years. They felt acutely their former employers' failure to recognize the long-term contribution they had made. Their resentment led to the development of negative attitudes. These attitudes caused invisible barriers to arise, and these barriers hindered them from securing other forms of employment. They began to suffer from lowered self-esteem. Their anger over their rejection increased their feelings of insecurity; and the days became filled with a lonely brooding (i.e., depression) over what had happened to them.

Feelings of rejection due to the denial of approval, affection, or recognition are hard to overcome. The inner anguish is very acute. If these feelings are not handled appropriately, problems, begin to multiply; and we must learn from our yesterdays if we are to face our tomorrows with confidence.

Through our study of the Bible we learn not only what happens in a typical "rejection syndrome," but also what we may do to avoid it. Cain[1] (see Gen. 4:1-16) is a good illustration of the former, while Samuel is an excellent example of the latter.

The People Request a King
1 Samuel 8:1-5

In contrast to Cain, whose rejection was first imagined and then self-inflicted, there is Samuel. In 1 Samuel 8 we read that the elders of Israel gather together and come to Samuel at Ramah; they say to him, *Behold, you have grown old and your sons do not walk in your ways. Now, appoint a king for us to judge us like the other nations* (8:5).

The rationale of the elders is clear. Samuel is old, too old in their estimation, to be able to carry on effectively as their leader. The help he had been to the nation in the past, his life-long service, and all the benefits they have enjoyed under his leadership, are now forgotten.

To be sure, Samuel may not have been as aware of his shortcomings as were some of the people. But to eject him from his office of judge solely on account of his age is the height of ingratitude. While his sons may not have been fit replacements for him, putting him out of office was not the answer. Israel was a *theocracy* and Samuel was God's chosen representative. To reject him was to reject God's government of them through His appointed delegate. And to ask for a king to guide them was to imply that God, their rightful King, had let them down.

The request of the elders is also clear, *We want a king so that we can be like the other nations* (8:19,20).

It had always been God's intention to give them a king,[2] a man after His own heart, when Samuel was dead. Instead of waiting for His appointed time they demand a king now. Their request is premature and they will not listen to Samuel as he tries to reason with them. His administration lacks ostentation and the benefits of his superintendence are overlooked. The people lose sight of the real reason for their success and begin comparing themselves with those about them. Instead of being thankful for the blessings of Samuel's leadership, they look askance at his bodily form. The result is the rejection of one of the greatest leaders of all time. As Matthew Henry so clearly pointed out, Samuel "looked mean in the eyes of those who judged by outward appearance; but a king in purple robes with his guards and officers of state would look great. "

Samuel Overcomes Rejection
1 Samuel 8:6-22

It is important for us to notice that Samuel immediately takes matters to the Lord. The request of the people is displeasing to him but he does not argue with them.

In overcoming rejection, Samuel first lays the whole matter before the One who had commissioned him to lead His people (8:6-8). In doing so he obtains a new perspective on his problem. He is also able to reassure himself of his standing before the Lord. His prayer places him in touch with the Person who is of far more emotional significance to him than the elders of Israel.

In Samuel's attitude and actions we have the secret of overcoming rejection. By means of prayer we are able to discuss everything with the Lord. We are able to tell Him exactly how we feel and why! Through prayer, if we are

37

entirely open and honest before the Lord, we obtain an entirely new perspective in our problem. And this kind of praying keeps us from harboring resentment and blaming others for the situation we find ourselves in. Furthermore, as a result of prayer we are given new directions.

A few years ago a mission leader spent time in great perplexity before the Lord. Later, in telling the experience, he said, "The first hour I spent telling God how frustrated I was with the young man who had come to work on the mission station. I had prayed for a suitable person to help with the work. To my chagrin the young man started taking over. I felt pushed out. Tensions developed and arguments became common. I was considering sending him back to the States.

"Before doing so, however, I decided to make it a matter of special prayer. As I prayed God began to show me that I was in the way. He had other plans for the mission. I was not a good administrator even though I had been superintendent for many years. My young assistant was more suited to control the details of the mission.

"As I prayed, God showed me that there was a new mission station He wanted opened. He had directed this young man to the mission for the specific purpose of taking the administrative duties from me. I was concerned with maintaining the status quo. I had not waited on the Lord for directions as had been my habit earlier in my ministry. Had I done so, the difficulties which we had experienced might never have arisen."

Following a period of intense prayer this mission leader obtained a new perspective on his problem and new directions for the mission. The young subordinate God sent his way proved to be ideal for the task at hand. From that time onwards the work progressed and everything ran smoothly.

As Samuel prays God is able to encourage him (8:7). *They have not rejected you*, the Lord reminds him, *but they have rejected Me.* Samuel is kept from harboring resentment when he finds how he stands with God in the matter.[3] This gives him an entirely new perspective on his problem and also takes the sting out of his rejection.

Samuel also receives explicit instructions from the Lord. *Now then listen to their voice; however, you shall solemnly warn them . . . of the way in which their king will treat them when he reigns over them.* How different from our experience when we reprimand others first and pray later!

And rising from prayer Samuel does as the Lord commanded him. He faithfully relates to the people all that God has told him (8:10-18). The people, however, are obstinate. They have set their hearts on having a king and insist that Samuel appoint one for them. In this connection it is important to note that the request of verse 5 has now become a demand. The people are deaf to reason. Their attitude is one of self-will and ingratitude.

In Samuel's response to the people we have the second principle in the art of handling rejection. *He willingly submitted himself to the will of God (8:9) and patiently bore the ingratitude of the people.* He did not complain even though such an expression of his feelings might have been justified. He drew his strength from his relationship with the Lord. He realized afresh that the only thing that mattered was what God thought of him. This took the sting out of their rebuff.

As we analyze the demand the Israelites made (8:19,20), we find that they were motivated by a desire for status. They wanted to be like the other nations. Their request shows their immaturity. They had forgotten that their very glory was to be different from the other nations. It was their privilege to have God rule over them. In this respect these Israelites were like many Christians today. We are prone to forget that we are a chosen generation, a holy nation, a royal priesthood and a peculiar people whose bodies are the temple of the Holy Spirit. All too often we want to conform to the standards of the world and forget that ours is a greater honor, a higher privilege and a nobler calling.

Implicit in the demand of the Hebrews for a king, there is the idea that they will benefit from the added prestige of having him judge them. They also hope that he will afford them protection and fight their battles. All of this may have been motivated by a realization that the Philistines were increasing in strength and would one day constitute a threat to their national well-being.

In demanding a king, however, they completely repudiate the benefits of Samuel's ministry (see 1 Sam. 7:13) and ignore the way in which he has conducted himself before them (see 1 Sam. 12:2-5). They reject him as if he is unworthy to continue in office, and request that he appoint a replacement that will be acceptable to them. Unwittingly, they have usurped the place of God and believe that they are the best judges of what is right for the nation.

Samuel's experience has a contemporary ring to it. There are many today who, as they near retirement, find that their sacrificial service is denied the recognition that should crown an honorable career. They are turned out of office while the administration makes room for others who are young and whose gifts and abilities may not have been proved. Even in Christian circles pastors frequently are set aside while the popular clamor is for something modern that will appeal to the senses. This desire for the ostentatious and fashionable invariably leads to a decline in spiritual fervor and, in the final analysis, proves less beneficial than that which God had appointed.

A third principle may be gleaned from our study of Samuel and the way in which he handles the situation. *Samuel faced ingratitude* (8:21,22). Ingratitude is as hard to bear as rejection, and Samuel knows of only one thing to do. He again takes matters to the Lord in prayer. Only in prayer, as he pours out his heart to God, can he find the peace he needs. He repeats all the words of the people in the ears of the Lord even though God knows perfectly well all that has

40

taken place. As in the previous instance God gives further directions to him.

It is important for us to observe that Samuel's prayer does not change the situation. So often when we pray we expect God to suddenly and miraculously bring about changes in our circumstances. We are then disappointed when He does not. The key to Samuel's handling of this emotionally charged situation lay in the fact that he submitted his will to the will of God. The problem then became the Lord's and he allowed Him to bear the burden. Samuel also allowed God to speak to him. And God allowed the people to have a king, since they were so inordinately set upon it.

The quality of Samuel's personality may be seen from the fact that he remained loyal to the people of Israel in spite of their rejection of him. His role was reduced, but his lightened responsibilities gave him the opportunity to spend time training young men in the "schools of the prophets."

The Crucible

As we review Samuel's situation, we find that God allows trials—even the trial of rejection—to come our way in order to refine us. He does not, however, abandon us to our fate, or watch from the sidelines to see what we will do. With each trial He makes provision for us so that we can be "winners" in spite of the difficulties we face (see 1 Cor. 10:13).

The way in which God helped Samuel face the ordeal of rejection and took the sting out of ingratitude is most instructive. As is so often the case, there was a definite role Samuel played in the drama and a definite part God undertook. Samuel's duty was to take the whole matter to the Lord and wait on Him for direction. There are some things that can only be accomplished by prayer! As Francois Fenelon observed, we should "talk to Him in prayer of all our

41

wants, our troubles ... we cannot speak too freely, too trustfully to Him."

In facing rejection our primary temptation is to accept the other person's estimate of us and adopt his system of values. When this happens we become a yo-yo on someone else's string. If we are passive individuals, this results in helpless apathy. We feel that we are of no value because our "worth" has been determined by another; and this other person has set us aside. And having tacitly approved the other person's system of values, we become "sympathy seekers," or try to manipulate others in order to receive attention.

In aggressive individuals there will be open resentment, a hostile exchange of words, and perhaps even violence.

Among moderates—those who neither passively accept nor angrily refuse the judgment of those who have rejected them—there is, nevertheless, the gnawing bitterness which, regardless of how well it may be concealed, ultimately shows itself in snide comments and derogatory remarks.

Regardless of whether we are passive, moderate, or aggressive in our handling of rejection, if we accept another's values, the outcome leads to the same conclusion: loneliness, bitter recrimination, and self-justifying sorties into the past.

The solution to this kind of situation is conceptually simple, though difficult to put into practice because we have grown accustomed to handling our feelings in different ways. In the case of Samuel *he refused to accept the external value system of the leaders.* He took the whole matter to the Lord in prayer. He found how he stood in God's eyes. This restored his confidence in himself and preserved his self-esteem.

In addition, in handling rejection *Samuel maintained a proper perspective on the problem.* He objectively analyzed the criticism of others. He avoided being caught on the continuum of "they're good, I'm bad," or *vice versa.* He learned that the elders were in reality rejecting God's rule over them.

Samuel was able to maintain his emotional equilibrium because *he gave God the opportunity to stabilize his feelings.* He was still God's servant and would continue to serve the Lord as long as he lived.

It is important for us, in our handling of situations such as this, to have a clear understanding of reality if we are to handle rejection properly. Our inability to comprehend the spiritual dimension of life has been described by Dr. William R. Inge. He asks, rhetorically, "If we spent 16 hours a day dealing with tangible things and only five minutes a day dealing with God, is it any wonder that tangible things are 200 times more real to us than God?"[4]

Samuel found that the reality of his relationship with God sustained him. He knew the importance of prayer. Without such communion the world would have gradually crowded God out of his life.[5]

Our fellowship with God—fellowship involving our minds, emotions and wills—will lift us above the transient things of time and sense. We will be able to experience true worthwhileness within God's value system. And only this kind of experience can sustain us in many of the varied experiences of life (see Rom. 8:37). As we shall see, it kept Samuel from jealousy when he was commissioned to appoint his successor.

Interaction

1. Why is rejection (in any of its forms) so hard for us to bear?
2. Contrast the experience of Cain (see Gen. 4:1-16; see footnote 1) with Samuel's handling of the situation which faced him. What principles emerge? How do they apply to situations we may face?
3. In what specific ways does submission to God's sovereignty make handling the difficulties of life easier? How does this differ from fatalistic resignation?

4. Why is ingratitude frequently linked with one or more forms of rejection?

5. Samuel's response to rejection and ingratitude was *prayer*. What may we learn from (a) his attitude and example, (b) the content of his prayers, and (c) God's response?

Footnotes

1. Cain's "rejection" was the result of disobedience. God had revealed to Adam what kind of sacrifice was acceptable to Him. Adam obviously passed this information on to his children, for Abel knew what offering to bring before the Lord. Cain, Abel's older brother, was a "produce farmer" (not a "cattle rancher" like Abel), and he disdained to ask a lamb of his younger brother. He rejected what he knew to be right and offered instead a sacrifice of "the fruit of the ground" to the Lord. When God refused to honor his sacrifice, Cain felt rejected.

The very fact that Cain's facial expression fell indicates that he was already suffering from feelings of guilt and lowered self-esteem. God, however, was not willing to abandon Cain. He gave Cain the opportunity to discuss his feelings. *"Why are you angry?"* He asked. *"And why has your glance fallen? If you do well, will not [your glance] be lifted up? And if you do not do well, sin is crouching [as a beast] at the door; and its desire is for you, but you must master it."*

In inviting Cain to discuss his feelings, God gave Cain an opportunity to benefit from his reactions and set things right. But Cain would not admit his error, nor would he offer the proper sacrifice. He wanted acceptance with God on his own terms. He did not ask for forgiveness, and, as a result, was left in bitterness and disillusionment. Three courses of action were open to him. He could turn the hurt inward and inflict it on himself. This would have made him feel even more guilty. In time the hurt he felt might have made him feel that he had atoned for what he had done wrong. In reality, however, his relationship with the One whom he felt had rejected him would have remained unchanged. To turn his anger inward would only have increased his feelings of unworthiness. And if these were not dealt with, they would ultimately have led to depression.

On the other hand, Cain could attempt to handle his feelings of hurt by projecting his anger outward. He could blame his damaged emotions on someone or something else. This is a childish way of handling the situation, but it is surprising how many grown people resort to it. It may help us live with ourselves, but in the final analysis it destroys our relationships with others. The result is loneliness and despair.

Cain chose to project his anger outward. He was, in reality, angry at God—the authority figure for rejecting him—but he was also afraid of God. God was too powerful for him. Not being prepared to admit his error, he

44

looked for an object on which to vent his animosity; and he found Abel! The Hebrew text is most interesting. It reads: *And Cain said to Abel his brother,* —. *And it came to pass when they were out in the field, that Cain rose up against Abel his brother and killed him* (Gen. 4:8). How revealing! Cain was unable to give expression to his feelings. His resentment was so great that he became incoherent. He lacked the sophistication with which we today cover our feelings. Anger, however, is still the same. The person who is angry is always right in his own eyes!

The final act in this drama of Cain's imagined rejection took place when God appeared to him the second time. *"Where is Abel your brother?"* He asked. To this Cain retorted, "I do not know." This was a denial of any knowledge of what had happened. And having first projected blame for his rejection on Abel, Cain now projected blame for Abel's murder on God. *"I'm not my brother's keeper,"* he replied. In saying this, he implied: You're wrong to even question me about him. And Cain went out of the presence of the Lord and journeyed as far away as he could. His improper reaction toward his imagined rejection (a) warped his perspective on life, (b) caused him to blame other people for his wrongdoing, (c) led to a loss of concern for the rights of others, (d) defiance of God, and (e) ultimately, to feelings of loneliness, insecurity, and further rebellion.

The third method of handling rejection would have necessitated that Cain submit to the authority of God. This he was unwilling to do.

2. See Genesis 17:6,7; 49:10; Deuteronomy 17:6,14,15; 28:36; Psalm 2:6; Isaiah 9:6,7; 11:1-9. It was always God's intention that the Davidic Kingdom would culminate in the Lord Jesus Christ (see 2 Sam. 7:8-17; Luke 1:32,33). This part of God's program, however, is still future (see Rev. 20:4; 1 Cor. 15:24).

3. The same principle holds true today. (See John 15:18-20; Colossians 1:24.) W.G. Blaikie's comments in *The First Book of Samuel*, pp. 114,115, are well taken.

4. W.R. Inge, *Faith and Its Psychology* (London: Duckworth, 1911), p. 74.

5. In *The Social Construction of Reality* (Garden City, NY: Doubleday, 1966), P.O. Bergen and T. Luckmann make the observation that our social identity and world view are created and maintained by conversation and interaction. If this is true on the human plane, it is even more important on a spiritual level. We need to spend time talking to the Lord and studying His Word if we are to develop our spiritual identity and a biblical world view.

PROGRAMMED FOR GREATNESS

1 SAMUEL 9:1—10:27

C.S. Lewis once remarked, "Anxiety is not only a pain we must ask God to assuage but also a weakness we must ask him to pardon."[1] He was speaking of the fear which we have all experienced—a fear which robs us of our peace and prevents us from giving of our best. While it is easy for us to echo the words of Franklin D. Roosevelt, "The only thing we have to fear is fear itself," the fact remains that anxiety is one of the most debilitating emotions. It is the opposite of trust and, if not properly controlled, leads to feelings of inadequacy, self-pity and depression.

In the continuing struggle between fear and faith, anxiety and confidence, worry and assurance, *internal* and *external* forces play a major role. These dynamics are illustrated for us in Saul. He had everything going for him; and yet, in spite of the fact that he had been anointed by Samuel, and had received signs confirming his election, when the time arrived for his presentation to the people his courage failed him (1 Sam. 10:22).

Choosing a King
1 Samuel 9:1—10:1

As we read of the events which led up to the selection of Saul to be Israel's king, we find that the Israelites have grown tired of the rule of the judges. They have looked about them and have seen that the surrounding nations have kings for leaders. Furthermore, the Philistines have established garrisons within their borders (see 10:5), and the Ammonites are beginning to threaten the tribes on the east of the River Jordan (see 12:12). The leaders believe that now is the time for a change. They want a figurehead they can see; one who can give them the leadership and prestige the other nations seem to enjoy.

In a most important chapter (see 1 Sam. 8) the sons of Israel make their request known to Samuel. The selection of a man to be their king takes place in a most remarkable way (1 Sam. 9). As we read about it we are introduced, for the first time, to Saul.

Saul's father is a leader of the tribe of Benjamin. Some of his donkeys are missing and, with a servant, Saul is sent to look for them. He searches vainly for the missing animals and, having been gone some time, is on the verge of giving up the search. Inasmuch as they are near Ramah, his servant suggests that they should visit Samuel and inquire of him about the missing donkeys (9:6-10).

As Saul and his servant enter the city, they see some young women going out to draw water. They ask them of Samuel's whereabouts, and they[2] are told that Samuel has recently returned from one of his missions (see 1 Sam. 7:16,17; 9:12) and is even now going to the place of sacrifice.

Saul and his servant hasten on up the hill. There they see an old man. Unaware that he is the one whom they are seeking, they ask him for directions to the seer's house. Samuel identifies himself and assures them that the donkeys have been found. He then instructs Saul and his servant to go on to the feast and promises to join them shortly. He also intimates that great things lie in store for Saul (9:15,16,20,21).

Following the feast Samuel entertains Saul. Before retiring for the night the prophet spends time with the young farmer (9:25). He undoubtedly discusses with him the solemn responsibilities which accompany God's choice of him as the new leader. As William G. Blaikie has pointed out, "Samuel could not but communicate to Saul the treasured thoughts of his lifetime regarding the way to govern Israel." He would have recalled God's purpose for His people, His providential dealings with Israel in the past, and the need for maintaining the theocracy (i.e., God's rule of His people through Saul). Dr. Blaikie goes on to emphasize the fervor with which Samuel would urge Saul to be faithful in observing the Law and maintaining the covenant relationship between God and His people. "The new king," he says, "would be tempted like all the kings around him, to regard his own will as the only rule of action, and to fall in with the prevalent notion that kings are above the law."[3] Self-seeking, however, would bring upon him the disciplining hand of God; submission would result in blessing (see 1 Sam. 2:30).

In the morning Samuel accompanies Saul to the gates of the city. He asks Saul to send his servant on ahead of them, and there he anoints Saul a *nagid*, "prince," over Israel.[4] Even though Saul will be replacing him as leader of his people, Samuel shows no sign of jealousy. He is anxious for Saul to succeed and is perfectly prepared to confine himself to a more limited role.

The choice of a king from the small tribe of Benjamin is most judicious. The tribes of Judah and Ephraim are the largest. They flank Benjamin on the north and the south.

If a man had been chosen from either of these two tribes, jealousy would have been sure to be the result.

Confirming the Choice
1 Samuel 10:2-16

Such sudden and dramatic events need confirmation, particularly to one of Saul's temperament. Samuel therefore gives Saul three signs. They will take place in a specified sequence and in designated places. His return to Gibeah will, for this reason, not be by the most direct route. It will involve some seemingly needless detours.[5]

The first sign will take place at Rachel's tomb (see Jer. 31:15). There Saul will meet two men who will tell him that the donkeys have been found (1 Sam. 10:2). Their independent testimony will confirm Samuel's own words and strengthen Saul's confidence in the Lord.

The second sign will be given him at "the oak of Tabor." There he will meet three men enroute to Bethel (10:3). They will give him two loaves of bread. It is a token of their homage and is a further indication of the way the Lord is preparing the hearts of His people to receive Saul.

The third sign is to occur at Gibeath-Elohim, "the hill of God," the seat of the Philistine governor[6] (see 1 Sam. 13:2, 3). There Saul will meet a group of prophets coming down from the high place. They will be singing and Saul will join them in giving thanks and praising the Lord. This time the Spirit of the Lord will come upon him and he will become a changed man.[7] He will no longer have the nature of a farmer but will be given the ability of a military leader (10:11,12).

All this happens exactly as Samuel predicted.

Controlled by God

It is impossible for us to read this story without seeing how minutely all the events are controlled by God. Each person acts in complete freedom. The result is an example of "divine logistics" (or providence), and serves to show us how perfectly God rules and overrules in the affairs of men to accomplish His purpose.

God's superintendence of events may be seen in the fact that Kish's donkeys went astray at the precise time Israel was seeking a king. Kish sent Saul, not one of the other members of his household, after the asses. In looking for the donkeys Saul made a wide circuit which led him to Ramah, the city of Samuel. While Saul was ignorant of the prophet's whereabouts and appearance (see 1 Sam. 9:18, 19), his servant happened to know that this was the residence of "the man of God."

In the outworking of the plan of God, Saul and his servant happened to arrive at Ramah on the day Samuel returned from one of his preaching missions. A day earlier and they might have returned home without seeing the prophet. They also happened to meet women going out of the city to draw water who had passed Samuel as he went up the hill to the feast. And after Samuel anointed Saul and sent him home, Saul met the men of whom Samuel spoke— in the specified sequence and without their being aware of what had taken place between the prophet and the newly-anointed king.

And so we might go on. Sufficient for us to notice that in every instance the people concerned acted without the slightest pressure. They were unaware of the fact that, behind the scenes, God was working to accomplish His purpose.

All of this should be of great encouragement to us. God's unseen involvement in our affairs—in our chance contacts as well as in the trials and disappointments of life—should give us confidence to trust Him with our todays as well as our tomorrows (see Rom. 8:28).

Unfortunately, Saul was not conscious of God's work in his life. He was externally oriented and was never persuaded of spiritual realities for very long.

Conflict over Approval
1 Samuel 10:17-27

Within a very short time Samuel gathers all the people together at Mizpah (10:17-25). He wishes them to witness firsthand God's appointment of their king. At Mizpah he brings each tribe before the Lord. When selection is made, the tribe of Benjamin is singled out. The families of the tribe then come near and the Matrite family is chosen. Finally, Saul, the son of Kish, is selected. But he is nowhere to be found. On further inquiry, God indicates that the new king is hiding among the baggage. Some people run to the carts and other gear and, when they have found him, they bring him before the people. The people are deeply impressed with Saul's appearance. He is taller than anyone else, and with shouts of *Long live the king!* (10:24) he is hailed as their new leader.

A group of resolute men accompany Saul to his house at Gibeah (10:26) and form his bodyguard. But there is also ready-made opposition. Certain worthless men (sons of Belial [10:27]) reject his appointment. They despise him and will not bring him the usual tokens of homage. They show by their actions the real state of their own hearts. In their rejection of Saul, they are also rejecting the theocracy he now represents. Saul, however, turns a deaf ear to their taunts.

Portrait of a Loser

But why did Saul's life lack spiritual perception? What caused him to hide among the baggage?

Psychological studies show that a person's reactions to a particular situation are invariably built up over a long period of time. For example, if a person has had a series of bad experiences with dogs, his reaction to a new encounter will be conditioned by his past recollections.

A careful assessment of the evidence given us about Saul —evidence about his home life and the way he had grown accustomed to think about himself—will provide us with an explanation for his hiding among the baggage. Our assessment of his background will reveal that Saul had lived too long in the shadow of his father's dominant personality. He was ignorant of spiritual matters and, as a result, had no resources outside of himself to draw on.

Saul's father, Kish, is spoken of as a *gibbor*, or *mighty man of valor* (1 Sam. 9:1). In an era of loose tribal federation and powerful enemies on all sides, a man had to be able to protect his family and lands if he was to survive. Kish had evidently excelled as a commander of the local militia, and had become one of the leaders of his tribe. He was so successful that in the course of time the people of his tribe bestowed on him the highest honor possible: he was referred to as a *gibbor*.

Saul's early life had evidently been dominated by his father. *He developed fear of one in a superior position.* Those who are accustomed to giving commands to a rough and ready group of volunteers, and punishing the slightest disobedience with despotic power, do not necessarily make kind and compassionate husbands and fathers. In contrast to Samuel's mother (who is spoken of in praiseworthy terms), Saul's mother is not mentioned. The probability is that, when her husband was at home, she and the children spent their time catering to his demands. It is not uncommon for children, who have grown to adulthood in austere, loveless surroundings, to concentrate their attention on satisfying as quickly as possible every wish of the dominant member of the household. Their well-being and emotional survival require it.

Evidence of Kish's disregard of Saul may be seen from the fact that he sent him on a menial errand. To be sure, donkeys were valuable creatures in those days, but such an errand could easily have been trusted to someone else. Apparently Saul was so used to being treated as a servant[8] that he obeyed his father's instructions without question.

But this kind of treatment bred in him a type of mental and emotional numbness. Happiness was probably equated with being away from home, or "a night out with the boys." And the tragedy of it is that as Saul grew to manhood he was unable to exercise proper initiative. He was far too accustomed to following orders. Our story confirms his lack of voluntary forethought, for insufficient food was taken on the journey; on approaching Ramah, Saul was penniless, and he readily followed his servant's suggestions.

A further indication of Kish's influence on his son may be seen from the fact that when Saul's servant suggests that they visit Samuel, Saul's immediate reaction is in reference to a father-figure. *We have nothing to bring him* (1 Sam. 9:7), he says. He obviously stands in awe (and perhaps dread) of anyone in a superior position.

But fear of anyone in a superior position is not the only thing Saul suffers from. *He is devoid of any internal God-consciousness.* This lack may also be attributed to his father. Kish's outlook on life was entirely materialistic. He and his family could not have engaged in any of the regular feasts (see Deut. 16:16), for Saul was completely ignorant of the prophet's existence. And Saul must have followed in the footsteps of his father's religious indifference even though, at the time of the story, he was a grown man (1 Sam. 13:1-3).

This view receives tacit confirmation from Saul himself. When he speaks of the Lord he uses the general term for God, *Elohim*, not *Yahweh*, "LORD," the name implying a relationship to the God of the covenant. As a result of his contact with Samuel, Saul soon learns the vocabulary. Subsequent references show that he does use the term *Yahweh*, LORD (see 1 Sam. 14:34,36-42; 19:6; 23:21; 24:17-19; 28:9,10), but there is no evidence of any commitment of himself to the conditions of the covenant. In this respect he is similar to many churchgoers today who, when they are with Christians, quickly pick up the traditional jargon but are slow to appreciate its true meaning.

Further evidence of Saul's unspiritual state is borne out in chapter 10. When he meets with the prophets and experiences the Spirit of God coming upon him, he joins them in their songs of thanksgiving. So dramatic is the reversal of roles that the people who know him exclaim in surprise, *What has happened to the son of Kish? Is Saul also among the prophets?* (1 Sam. 10:11). And from that time onwards, they use this incident to describe what is most unlikely to happen.

Saul's whole manner of life is governed by external considerations. As a result, spiritual realities make no lasting impact on him. When he is not constantly in touch with people who feed his internal orientation with their own spiritual dynamic he lapses back into his old ways and his confidence in the Lord wanes.

Influence of External Pressures

We are all susceptible to external influences. Our daily contact with the world, the traffic of new ideas through our minds, and the constant bombardment of things directed at our senses, all detract from our inner awareness of God and His presence. The story of Saul illustrates the way in which external considerations may dominate our lives.

Pressure of our senses. The Israelites, for example, wanted the prestige of having a king to rule over them. They came to Samuel with their request. At Mizpah, when Saul was presented to them, they were impressed with his outward appearance (1 Sam. 10:22-24). He appealed to them. Unfortunately, their assessment of him was governed by their senses. Their motivation was external and secular; and God gave them exactly what they asked for.

Pressure of materialism. A further illustration of how external pressures influence our actions may be found in the case of Kish. He was concerned over the disappearance of his donkeys and sent his son to look for them. Saul made a wide circuit as he searched for them. By comparison, Ramah, where Samuel lived, was a stone's throw away; but there is no evidence that Kish was ever concerned enough over his son's spiritual well-being to send him to worship at the sanctuary. His motivation was materialistic.

Pressure of matrimonial considerations. Then there were the girls of Ramah. If the Talmud is correct, they would gladly have detained Saul and conversed with him. They were attracted to his outward appearance. Their reaction to him was perfectly natural and there may not have been too many eligible young men in Ramah. They were motivated by matrimonial considerations.

Pressure of fear. Saul was a product of his times. Having a strong external orientation, it is no wonder that in the interval between his anointing and his presentation to the people, his confidence wavered. He became anxious and worried. Fear began to rise in his heart. How could he lead these people? Would his appointment end in failure? His fear narrowed his perception until God's confirmatory signs were forgotten. He spent time thinking about the awesome prospect before him instead of seeking a solution. Realizing his own insufficiency he never reached out and invoked the aid of the Lord. Instead, he developed a mindset. God had given him everything he needed to succeed. He could have been a "winner." Saul, however, could only perceive of himself in terms of his past. And when the time came for him to be presented to the people, he hid among the baggage.

Portrait of a Winner

In contrast to the morbid anxiety of an externally oriented person (see Prov. 12:25; Isa. 26:3), there is the encouragement the Lord Jesus gives those who reach out to Him.

In a passage of Scripture which has become so familiar to us that its real message is largely overlooked (Matt. 6:24-34), the Lord Jesus instructs us not to be overly anxious about the things of this life—what we shall eat, what we shall drink, what we shall put on—for the Father cares for us! As we realize more of His unchanging love for us, we can take confidence from the fact that He continues to watch over us. First, *we belong to Him* (see Eph. 2:19) by ties that can never be severed (see Rom. 8:31-39).

Second, *we have value* (see Matt. 6:26). We are not only sons of God, but we have also been made His heirs (see Rom. 8:17; Gal. 3:29; Titus 3:7). We have an inheritance that no one can take from us (see Eph. 1:11; Col. 3:24; 1 Pet. 1:4). Saul lacked this sense of worth. He thought of himself as being little better than a slave. This distorted his vision. Never having achieved any measure of success he anticipated failure and hid from those who would make him king.

Third, in the providence of God, *we are made equal to the task*. He has given the gift of the Holy Spirit to all who put their trust in the Lord Jesus. He indwells us (see John 14:16,17) and *He enables us* to do what we could not do without His help (see Gal. 5:16-20; John 14:12). The Spirit had come on Saul equipping him for the task ahead. Saul, unfortunately, was so externally oriented he did not appreciate what God had done for him. As a result, he hid among the baggage.

In His marvelous plan for us God sees fit to give us the very things we may have missed in childhood (see Col. 2:9,10). *We belong to Him*, *we are of value* before Him (see John 4:10), and *we are made* (competent) *equal to every task* (see Phil. 4:13). All of this does not mean that we will not experience anxiety or fear. We will! Our background and conditioning (like the person who had only bad experiences with dogs) will betray us time and again (see Rom. 8:5). But as we grow spiritually and daily learn more of God's provision for our lives, trust will begin to replace fear and apprehension will give way to confidence. Furthermore, as we learn how to recognize our emotional reactions

56

and draw on God's unfailing resources, we will be led in a constant pageant of triumph (see 2 Cor. 2:14).

Interaction

1. T.S. Eliot observed: "The obvious secularist solution for a muddle is to subordinate everything to political power." This idea lay at the root of Israel's demand for a king. What alternatives were there? Why were they ignored?

2. Take a concordance (such as Strong's *Exhaustive Concordance to the Bible*) and, by looking up words such as "carnal" and "flesh" on the one hand, and "spiritual" on the other, make a list of the different ways these characteristics are manifested. What does this teach us about externally and internally oriented people?

3. To what extent may the Holy Spirit's ministry in our lives counteract the detrimental influences of our childhood? What can we learn from Saul's situation that will help us make a positive impact on our children?

4. Samuel gave Saul three signs. What should he have learned from them?

5. After being in Samuel's presence, Saul exhibits some excellent characteristics (for example, humility and discretion; see 1 Sam. 10:14-16). List them. Why did his confidence fail him at Mizpah (1 Sam. 10:21-23)? What resources could he have used?

Footnotes

1. C.S. Lewis, *Mere Christianity* (New York: Macmillan, 1958).

2. The *Talmud* picks up the emphasis on "to them" inherent in the Hebrew text and suggests that the young women found Saul so handsome that if his business had not been so pressing they would have tried to detain him in conversation.

3. Blaikie, *The First Book of Samuel*, p. 142.

4. The word *nagid* refers to Saul's rulership over God's people. It differs from *melek*, "king," in that it points to Saul's function rather than his

position. God had told Samuel that Saul would "have authority over" His people (1 Sam. 9:17). The word means "to restrain" and contrasts the "restraints of a settled government with the license of the time in which 'every man did what was right in his own eyes,' " A.F. Kirkpatrick, *The First Book of Samuel* (Cambridge: At the University Press, 1888), p. 108.

5. Alfred Edersheim, *The Bible History of the Old Testament* (Grand Rapids: Eerdmans, 1954), vol. 4, pp. 44-46; Yohanan Aharoni and Michael Avi-Yonah, *The Macmillan Bible Atlas* (New York: Macmillan, 1968), p. 86.

6. The word is *netsib*, and its meaning varies between "prefect," "garrison," and "pillar." The importance assigned to the city (the original contains the article) seems to point to Gibeah as being the residence of a Philistine official.

7. The question is frequently asked, Was Saul saved when God gave him "another heart"? A.R.S. Kennedy, in *Samuel: The Century Bible* (London: Caxton, n.d.), says, "His is the first conversion recorded in sacred literature." But such is not the view of modern scholars. It is preferable to conclude with A.M. Renwick that this experience turned Saul from a "rustic farmer's son into a statesman and warrior," *The New Bible Commentary* (Grand Rapids: Eerdmans, 1968), p. 269.

8. The text confirms this view. Notice the emphasis on "*us*" and "*we*" in 1 Samuel 9:5-10. Apparently Kish's overbearing manner had robbed Saul of all sense of self-worth.

A QUESTION
OF CREDENTIALS

1 SAMUEL 11:1—14:52

Saul, Israel's first king, has gone down in history as a tragic figure. He lacked conviction and was slow to initiate action. Instead, he waited for the pressure of external events to dictate a course of action to him, and this determined his world of reality.

As we read the events of 1 Samuel 11 through 14 we are given several interesting pictures of Saul. In chapter 11 we see him responding to a crisis—external pressure—and, by means of God's help, achieving a significant victory. In chapter 12 he and the people commemorate the victory, but in chapter 13 Saul is once more indecisive. Should he attack the Philistines or wait for them to attack him? Jonathan takes the initiative and wrests a military outpost from the hands of the invaders. This precipitates a crisis—a spiritual one—and Saul's faith is found to be deficient. Finally, in chapter 14, the bewildered king is seen sitting under a tree, not knowing what to do.

The First Call to Duty

1 Samuel 11:1-7

Chapter 11 is connected with the coronation of Saul by the word *Now* (11:1, *NASB*). Apparently, after Saul has been made king in Gilgal, he goes back to Gibeah. Instead of establishing himself as leader over God's people, he returns to farming. Then an event the elders of Israel had anticipated takes place (1 Sam. 12:12); trouble arises in the territory east of Jordan. Nahash, the Ammonite king, attacks Jabesh-Gilead. Setting aside their covenant relationship with the Lord, the people of Jabesh-Gilead state that they are willing to become Nahash's vassals.[1] Nahash, however, wants to humiliate all Israel and is not to be satisfied so easily (11:2)! He therefore proposes to gouge out the right eye of every inhabitant.

The men of Jabesh-Gilead obtain a week's respite and send messengers throughout Israel to try and obtain help. Elders from their tribe (Manasseh) have undoubtedly attended Saul's inauguration, but word of the appointment of the new king has not yet reached people in the towns and villages. Their messengers pass through Ephraim and, in their journey south, arrive in the territory of Benjamin. Upon learning the reason for their visit, the inhabitants of Benjamin give loud expression of their grief (11:3,4). None of them apparently give any thought to Saul. His appointment has made little impact on them.

It is while all this is taking place that Saul comes from the fields. Inquiring about the reason for the noise, he is told of Nahash's threat. The Spirit of God comes upon him. His anger wells up. Taking the oxen he was using to plow the field, he slaughters them on the spot. Then, sending messengers throughout Israel and Judah, he summons the people to Bezek (11:5-7).[2]

But why had Saul been inactive? What prevented him from setting up his headquarters and beginning to train his militia?

The only satisfactory answer seems to be that Saul did not know what to do. Following his coronation at Mizpah he returned to his farm. His indecision doubtlessly weighed heavily on him. He knew that something should be done, but what? Lacking any strong internal dynamic he returned to what he knew best and waited for outward circumstances to dictate a course of action to him.

God, however, had not forsaken Saul. When the king heard of Nahash's outrageous proposal the Spirit of the Lord came upon him. And the man who had hidden himself among the baggage at Mizpah arises to challenge Israel with the task of delivering their kinsmen.

But how are we to explain Saul's anger? The intensity, as well as the irrationality, of his response is in marked contrast to his former modesty and self-effacement.

Saul, apparently, was impulsive. Impulsiveness stems from immaturity which, in Saul's case, was probably a direct result of being so long dominated by his father. He evidently resented Kish's treatment of him but suppressed his feelings, for he dared not openly oppose his father. But harboring these ill feelings only made him inwardly angry. His anger was bottled up inside him until it found an outlet —in this instance the slaughter of the oxen.

Saul was probably unaware of the full implication of his impulsive action. It is not beyond the realm of possibility that, as Dorothy F. Zeligs stated, "In killing the oxen, Saul might have acted out the conquest of [his] father." Furthermore, "these animals may have represented an aspect of his own personality. Oxen are submissive [animals] ... who plow the soil in dull routine. By slaying them, Saul may have been [symbolically] overcoming the submissive element in his own personality."[3]

Then Saul sends messengers with pieces of the oxen throughout all the coasts of Israel and Judah, saying, *Whoever does not come out after Saul and after Samuel, so shall it be done to his oxen* (11:7).

A Significant Victory
1 Samuel 11:8-15

The people respond to Saul's summons and rally together at Bezek (11:8). Then under Saul's leadership they march on Nahash. In the half-light of early dawn they reach the Ammonite encampment. And there, perhaps remembering Gideon's strategy (see Judg. 7:16), Saul divides his men into three groups (11:11). Their attack comes as a complete surprise to the Ammonites. So confident are they of victory that Saul's men are within the camp before the guard realizes what is happening.

The routing of the Ammonites is complete. Even in flight they are unable to find a place where they can regroup their forces and make a stand (11:11). And Saul gains a significant victory!

Samuel had either accompanied the men to the scene of the battle, or else waited for them in Bezek; for on the return of the men from pursuing the Ammonites, he finds them aglow with the flush of their success. So enthused are they with their new leader that they turn on those who had initially opposed Saul's appointment: *Who is it that said, 'Shall Saul reign over us?' they ask. 'Bring these men, that we may put them to death'* (11:12).

Saul's response is magnanimous. He shows the generosity of his nature under the influence of the Spirit of God. *There shall not a man be put to death this day,* he says; *for the LORD has wrought deliverance in Israel* (11:13). And Samuel, acting to relieve the tension, summons all the people to Gilgal where they confirm Saul as king[4] and offer sacrifices to the Lord in acknowledgment of His goodness to them. The result is a time of great rejoicing.

All of this points to a most important fact: it is easy for externally oriented people to praise the Lord when everything is going well. Unfortunately, when the enthusiasm of the moment passes, or when something arises to detract from their euphoria, their zeal and dedication wane.

The Importance of Steadfastness
1 Samuel 12:1-25

Samuel is a wise leader. He realizes the need to challenge the people to follow the Lord even when there is no victory to celebrate. While everyone is in high spirits he takes the opportunity to impress on them the importance of stead-fastness (1 Sam. 12). In his address he first outlines his own conduct (12:1-5) and then recounts God's dealings with the people of Israel in the past (12:6-19). He warns them of the danger of apostasy and confirms his words by calling on God for rain. At that time of the year rain is unheard of and the people are overcome with fear at the sudden downpour. They entreat Samuel to pray that the Lord may be merciful to them (12:20-25).

But what was Saul doing while Samuel was addressing the people?

Recession of Hope—Externally-Oriented Person
1 Samuel 13:1—14:3

From what we observe in chapter 13, the effect of Samuel's exhortation on Saul must have been devastating. It seems as if Samuel's administration—an administration based on the prophet's integrity, coming directly from his relationship with God—caused Saul to have certain misgivings. Perhaps his feelings of inadequacy reasserted themselves. He realized that he did not have what was needed to follow in the old prophet's footsteps. Instead of taking courage from God's enablement (an enablement so recently demonstrated at Jabesh-Gilead), his joy evaporated. With downcast spirits he returned to Benjamin to make his headquarters in Michmash. There he seems to have been content to face the Philistine garrison across the ravine without attempting to repel them from the land.

This kind of experience is typical of externally-oriented people. They *lack the internal dynamic that will help them overcome depression*, but rely on situational pressure to give them direction. Having no internalized purpose, outward circumstances become their guide. The stronger the stimulus, the greater their response.

The problem with a person who lacks internal direction —whether a manager or foreman, husband or wife, teacher or coach, therapist or theologian—is that he fails to see the long-range consequences of his actions. In his indecision he appears flexible, but this "flexibility" is like a Sunday afternoon drive with no destination in mind. And being oriented to external impulses, his response is always dependent upon the way he perceives immediate reality. He may react or overreact, positively or negatively, with little or no consistency in his behavior.

Notice further that, as Saul listens to Samuel tell of God's dealings with Israel's past rebellion and sees the evidence of God's disapproval of them in the present (19-25), *he lacks the ability to discern his place in the divine plan.* God's anger is not directed at him, but against the people. If he follows the Lord he will continue to enjoy His blessing. Unfortunately, Saul's experience with a father-figure has been such that when any disapproval is voiced he instinctively withdraws to a place where he can be away from all authority. And in the biblical narrative he takes off for Michmash (not Gibeah). But being depressed as a result of Samuel's charge to the people, he imagines a personal rebuke and is paralyzed to the point of passivity. The gains of his recent victory over the Ammonites and his confirmation as king are all swept away.

Chapter 13 opens with a statement summarizing the length of Saul's reign.[5] It then describes the impasse which Saul faces at Michmash; an impasse which, by nature, he is not able to overcome. He chooses 3,000 men, divides them into two groups . . . and waits (13:2).

Inactivity is disastrous to externally-oriented people. In Saul's case he must have felt keenly his own lack of initiative. Unfortunately *he lacked the ability to institute action*

64

because he had no internal convictions or principles to guide him. He lacked the essence of good leadership. A leader must be a man "who can be looked up to, whose personal judgment is trusted, who can inspire and warm the hearts of those he leads . . . . Leadership is based on truth and character. A leader must himself be the servant of truth, and . . . he must have the force of character necessary to inspire others to follow him with confidence."[6]

Regrettably, Saul only exercised leadership when outward circumstances forced him to take action. He, therefore, waited for the Philistines to take the initiative (13:7).

Jonathan, as we shall see in a later chapter, has the inner characteristics his father lacks. He attacks the Philistine garrison[7] in Geba and kills the governor. The Philistines marshall a formidable army[8] and stage a reprisal. In accordance with Samuel's instructions (10:8), Saul withdraws to Gilgal to wait for Samuel.

Waiting is always difficult. For a person of Saul's temperament it was doubly hard, for he and those who were with him could daily watch vast numbers pour into the Philistine camp. The pressure mounts. Desertions among Saul's men increase. Finally, after an agonizing week, the seventh day dawns. But where is Samuel? What if he does not come? Perhaps he has been captured.

As the day wears on Saul becomes more concerned. If something doesn't happen soon he might not have enough men with which to fight. Finally, in desperation, he orders the offering to be brought to him. He feels compelled to go through with the ritual to assure himself of God's blessing. Only then can he engage the Philistines in battle.

The pressure of outward circumstances and the failure of Samuel to arrive in Gilgal at the appointed time goads Saul into disobeying the command of the Lord. *He lacks faith in God.* What he observes, namely, the growing strength of the Philistines, compels him to take action (13:9)! (After all, what use is faith without works?) But his actions only hide his lack of faith. He follows the dictates of his own reason rather than submit himself to the revealed will of God. God is testing him, and Saul is soon to find that obedience is the basic principle in His Kingdom. It is the portal to blessing. Gideon had already proved what God could do with 300 faithful men. Jonathan would later say, *The LORD is not restrained to save by many or by few* (14:6). And David, too, would follow this same principle when facing Goliath.

And so it is *fear* (not faith!) that drives Saul to offer the sacrifice.[9]

Saul has no sooner finished offering the burnt offering when Samuel arrives (13:10). Feeling that Samuel's presence will guarantee him victory, Saul goes out to welcome him. He is unprepared for the prophet's stern rebuke.

Gone now are all the good reasons for disobeying God's word. Saul's answer is weak: *I saw the people were drifting away from me,* he whines; *and you yourself had not come within the appointed time, and the Philistines were assembling at Michmash; therefore I said, 'Now the Philistines will come down to me at Gilgal, and I have not placated the LORD'; so I felt compelled to offer the burnt offering myself* (13:11).

How like us today! We feel that if we read our Bibles and pray every day, nothing unpleasant should befall us. And some of us believe that because we tithe we should be free of all economic adversity. We look upon our devotions or stewardship as the means whereby we may placate an angry deity. Our view of God is deficient. Trials and difficulties aid our growth. The difference is how we perceive God: as an angry deity or a loving Father. The former is a characteristic of externally-oriented people, and it breeds fear; the latter is the perspective of the internally-oriented, and it leads to confidence.

Samuel's rebuke of Saul places his actions in their correct perspective. By disobeying the command of the Lord he has shown himself unfit as a leader. As a consequence his *dynasty* will not continue (13:13,14). Samuel then returns to Gibeah and Saul is left with an army of 600 men. With the Philistines occupying their former encampment at Michmash, Saul establishes his new headquarters at Geba (13:16). In essence he offers a no-contest plea and avoids a battle.

Saul has taken Samuel's rebuke to mean the Lord's rejection of him personally. He thinks neither of repentance nor entreaty. The result is that at Geba there is a repetition of the circumstances which faced him first at Gibeah and then at Michmash. He feels sorry for himself. Fear reduces him to inactivity, and the overwhelming strength of the Philistines paralyzes him. He knows of the raiding bands that destroy the land but he does nothing to prevent them. The situation (from *his* perspective) seems hopeless. He feels frustrated. He knows the people look to him for help, but he is powerless to do anything. He becomes keenly aware of his loss of esteem in the eyes of his men. All he can do is sit under a pomegranate tree and brood over his sorrowful situation (14:2).

The passage before us mentions the presence of a priest with an ephod in Saul's camp (14:3). This is important because it shows that God had provided Saul with all he needed to confess his sin and seek His will. Saul, however, ignored these provisions.

Values in Conflict—Internally-Oriented Person
1 Samuel 14:4-52

Once again it is Jonathan who brings deliverance to the Israelites (14:4-15). Numbers are not important to him because his strength comes from the Lord. With his armor-bearer he attacks the Philistine garrison at Michmash. God works through him and the Philistines are routed. An Israelite watchman sees the commotion in the Philistine camp and tells Saul. A hasty roll call determines that Jonathan is missing. Rallying his men he heads for the field of battle (14:16-23).

Saul's leadership has suffered the natural consequences of lack of direction. He feels the need to reassert his authority. Realizing that he lost face religiously when he offered the sacrifice at Gilgal, he determines to regain some of his lost prestige by placing his men under a religious curse.[10] He extracts from them an oath to abstain from food during that day (14:24-30). His action is very revealing. It shows his rash impetuosity, desire for control, and superstitious turn of mind. He seems to believe that by abstaining from food the Israelites will, in some magical way, be guaranteed success. Unfortunately, through his indiscretion, his men become so weak from pursuing their enemies they are unable to capitalize on Jonathan's victory (14:31-35).

Jonathan is unaware of the command of his father and, seeing a beehive, he takes some of the honey (14:27). On learning of Jonathan's action, Saul's anger—the product of his recent frustration and loss of self-esteem—gushes out. He determines to show his power as a leader by executing his son (14:44). His decision is irrational; and gone is the former magnanimity which he displayed after delivering the people of Jabesh-Gilead (see 1 Sam. 11:12,13)! In giving the order for Jonathan to be put to death Saul succeeds only in further alienating his men. For the first time they refuse to obey him. Their response is dramatic: *Must Jonathan die, who has brought about this great deliverance in Israel? Far from it! As the LORD lives, there shall not one hair of his head fall to the ground, for he has worked with God this day* (1 Sam. 14:45). Such a response further weakens Saul's control. He had hoped to strengthen his position as their leader and now he is prevented from taking full advantage of Jonathan's success.

And each man returns to his own home (14:46).

One good thing comes of all this. Saul realizes the danger of inactivity. Now that the Israelites once more enjoy autonomy, he strengthens his position and then attacks his enemies on all sides (14:47,48). By taking the initiative, he avoids being cooped up as he was at Geba. As long as he is waging war and winning victories he can assert his authority. This helps him maintain the respect of his men. Continuous warfare also provides Saul with an outlet for his anger. By being active he can work off his tensions. The result is a period in which he gives of his best to his people.

In the final analysis we find that while externally-oriented people are apparently flexible, reactive rather than assertive, and largely dependent upon outward stimuli, they are also easily frustrated, and the anger they develop internally can erupt in irrational behavior. They come to rely heavily on others for approval and need continuous reinforcement if they are to give of their best.

How different is the experience of the internally oriented! *They walk by faith*, not by sight (see 2 Cor. 5:7). The ministry of the Spirit of God helps them overcome the tendency to rely on the flesh (see Rom. 8:4,5). Instead of being weak and vacillating *they are strengthened by the Spirit* in the inner man (see Eph. 3:16); and through the Holy Spirit's control *they are made a blessing to others*.

How tragic that Saul never yielded himself to the One who could have done so much through him. And equally as tragic is our experience if we fail to learn from his example and yield ourselves to Him who can accomplish so much through us (see Rom. 12:1,2). Conformity to His will continues to be the key to blessing.

Interaction

1. From our study of Saul, what would you conclude were the primary problems facing an externally-oriented person? Are we inclined to be like this? In what ways has our modern society reduced our awareness of these problems.?

2. In Romans 8:5 we read, *The fleshly [carnal] man sees no further than the carnal things of this life. But the spiritual man*

69

is concerned with the things of the Spirit. In what ways does this statement point out the difference in the administrations of Samuel and Saul?

3. What prompted Saul to order Jonathan's execution?

4. Why is waiting (for example, for prayers to be answered) so hard for externally-oriented people? What prompted Saul to offer the sacrifice at Gilgal? How may similar situations cause us to doubt God's involvement in our affairs? And how may these pressures prompt us to do the right thing in the wrong way, or try to help God achieve our will when patience and trust are what He requires?

5. A case history: A salesman has been extraordinarily successful. Under the pressure to produce he has led his company's roster of top agents year after year. In the course of time, however, he is promoted. Now it is his duty to set goals, motivate the sales force, attend committee meetings, and present reports to the executives of his company. While he was a success as a salesman, he is a failure as a manager. Some pressure is still present, but it is pressure of a different kind. What *internal* dynamics does he need in order to succeed?

Footnotes

1. In keeping with the milieu of the ancient Near East, Israel was under a "Suzerain," the Lord of glory, who appeared to them on Mount Sinai and constituted them a nation. He pledged His support to them provided they would obey His laws. Examples of this kind of treaty may be found in J.B. Pritchard's *Ancient Near Eastern Texts* (Princeton: Princeton University Press, 1959), p. 203; and D.J. Wiseman's *Vassal-Treaties of Esarhadon* (London: British School of Archaeology in Iraq, 1958). By agreeing to become the vassals of Nahash the men of Jabesh-Gilead in effect repudiated the covenant God had made with them. See W.G. Blaikie, *The First Book of Samuel*, p. 170.

2. *The Macmillan Bible Atlas*, p. 87.

3. See Dorothy F. Zeligs, *Psychoanalysis and the Bible*, p. 127. Saul, however, could only free himself from the control of Kish by placing himself

under a more powerful parental figure, namely, Samuel. This is why he links Samuel with himself in issuing the challenge of Israel.

4. The renowned German theologian, Rudolf Kittel, in *Great Men and Movements in Israel* (New York: Ktav. 1968), claims that in 1 Samuel we have conflicting manuscript evidence and three separate accounts of Saul's coronation. There is nothing in the biblical record to lead us to this conclusion. Saul's private anointing by Samuel was different from his public selection at Mizpah. And the importance of being confirmed as king is underscored by the fact that certain people had opposed his appointment.

5. The chronological problem associated with chapter 13:1 has been ably handled by John J. Davis in *Biblical Numerology* (Grand Rapids: Baker, 1968), pp. 86,87. Alfred Edersheim has an extensive footnote dealing with the same problem on page 56 of his work; and A.M. Renwich offers some plausible solutions in *The New Bible Commentary*, p. 269.

6. Bernard L. Montgomery, *The Path to Leadership* (London: Collins, 1961), pp. 10,11.

7. The Hebrew *netsib*, as we observed earlier, has a variety of meanings, one of which is "governor." It seems most likely that in the attack on Gega, Jonathan killed the Philistine governor.

8. Bible scholars are puzzled over the large number of chariots, etc., mentioned in the text. Alfred Edersheim offers a reasonable explanation in a footnote on p. 59 of his *Bible History*.

9. Some writers believe Saul's sin was his intrusion into the priestly office. However, sacrifices were offered by other men at a later time (e.g., David) without penalty. The Jewish commentator, S. Goldman, believes Saul's sin was "impatience": *Samuel* (London: Soncino Press, 1964), p. 72. It seems preferable to conclude that Saul was punished for his disobedience.

10. It is a well-established criterion that power in pagan cultures resides in the *power to curse*, while Judaism and Christianity alone possess the *power to bless*. Only in the Judeo-Christian religion is there emphasis on love and acceptance. Paganism creates a dogma of fear while the Bible emphasizes the grace and loving-kindness of God.

RULES OF THE GAME

1 SAMUEL 15:1—16:23

Benjamin Franklin once remarked: "He that cannot obey, cannot command!" As we study the life of Saul we see how, centuries ago, the Bible illustrated the truth of this New Englander's observation.

Obedience is one of the hardest lessons for us to learn. To disobey is natural (see Ps. 58:3). Our early actions as children were often marked either by a refusal to obey or negligence in carrying out a command. At times our parents chastened us. This was painful, but necessary. We needed to learn obedience before our self-will involved us and others in the consequences of our wrongdoing.

Disobedience, for the human race, began in the Garden of Eden. When Satan tempted Eve he started by casting doubt on God's goodness. He implied that restrictions were evil (see Gen. 3:1,6; compare with Gen. 2:16,17). By insinuating that God was wrong for having placed restrictions on them, Satan impugned the goodness of God. His second step was to cast doubt on the reliability of God's word (see Gen. 3:4). He implied that God had been keeping something from Adam and Eve. He had done it to frighten them (see Gen. 3:4,5). Eve was taken in by his guile, took of the fruit and gave some of it to Adam.

Unfortunately, disobedience always brings with it its own penalty. It begins by depriving us of God's blessing (see Deut. 28:15-51), and later blights the lives of others as well. In the case of Adam and Eve, their sin involved them and their descendants. They were expelled from the garden God had made for them (see Gen. 3:23,24), and the entire human race now shares in the consequences of their actions (see Rom. 5:12,17,19).

The real character of disobedience, however, is described by Samuel. He exposes the self-will inherent in resisting God's will and likens it to setting up ourselves as a *rival authority* to God. *Does the LORD have as great delight in burnt offerings and sacrifices*, he asks, *as in obeying the voice of the LORD? Behold, to obey is better than sacrifice, and to harken than the fat of rams. For rebellion is as the sin of witchcraft, and stubbornness is as iniquity and idolatry* (15:22,23).

Character of Saul's Disobedience
1 Samuel 15:10-23

As we take up our story of Saul and his disobedience it will be of help to us if we find out at what time of life the events described took place.

Saul is middle-aged. He is at that stage in life when his *family* is grown (see 1 Sam. 14:49), and as far as we know only two daughters remain unmarried (see 1 Sam. 17:25; 18:17,19,27). His *fortunes* have improved, and under his leadership Israel has prospered. Their enemies have been subdued (see 1 Sam. 14:47,48), and David will later say of him that he *clothed the daughters of Israel in scarlet [warmly][1] and put ornaments of gold on your apparel* (2 Sam.

1:24). And as for the *future*? Saul's anticipation of the future can only be understood in the light of his past. His years from boyhood to manhood were spent under the domination of his father (see 1 Sam. 9:1,2). He had grown to maturity being treated on the same level as a slave.[2] No matter how well he performed his work he never met with approval. As a consequence he developed an internal conception of himself which prosperity could not alter. He desperately craved praise and recognition. During his early years as king over Israel he was too busy to think of his own personal needs. Now, however, with the immediate concerns of his family and his people taken care of, his old unsatisfied longings reassert themselves. He is dominated now by a craving for fame and respect. However, in spite of all his victories, he remains unsatisfied. His people regard him as a national hero, but his leadership lacks an inspirational quality and he has not earned the respect of a *gibbor*, a "mighty man of valor." As a result no amount of outward successes can satisfy him.

This phenomenon is common to people in their 40s. Invariably, if they have been denied praise in their childhood, they crave it from friends and associates in middle life and will go to great lengths to achieve it. They will spend time and effort beautifying themselves or their homes, engaging in costly hobbies, "keeping up with the Joneses"—all with a view to winning the approval of others. As with Saul they lack *internal* structures to help them evaluate their own successes and give them a sense of personal satisfaction. And at the base of all this striving there is a lack of self-worth.

Those who do not learn how to cope with the dynamics of their own personalities in their 40s or early 50s will spend their future years looking backwards and sugar-coating the past—deriving satisfaction from nostalgic reminiscences—talking of the good old days, and trying to convince themselves that they were really successful.

Saul yearned for the kind of recognition and approval he was denied in his youth. He desperately wanted to be held in high esteem by his people. The problem he faced was that no amount of external success was ever sufficient to counteract his internalized image of himself as a failure. And coupled with this poor self-image was an innate fear of losing his popularity with the people (15:24). This basic fear led him to disobey God in the hope of gaining what he wanted most—the approval of others. Some indication of the inner workings of his personality—his basic desires as well as his fear of the people—may be seen from the following: (1) Saul never told the people that the spoils of war were to be totally destroyed (15:19); (2) he disobeyed the expressed command of God by taking Agag alive (15:8); (3) he erected a monument to commemorate *his* victory over the Amalekites (15:12; compare with 1 Sam. 7:12); and (4) he held special celebrations at Gilgal where he planned to parade Agag as a trophy of *his* military prowess.

Background of Saul's Disobedience
1 Samuel 15:1-9

When Samuel comes to Saul his opening statement emphasizes the gravity of the assignment God is entrusting him (15:1-3). The repetition of *LORD* and His covenant relationship with Israel should not be overlooked, and the stress on *LORD of hosts* indicates that God Himself will lead the assault.[3]

The instruction to Saul is very explicit:

I will punish Amalek for what he did to Israel, how he set himself against him on the way while he was coming up from Egypt. Now go and strike Amalek and utterly destroy all that he has, and do not spare him; but put to death both man and woman, child and infant, ox and sheep, camel and donkey (15:2,3).

God's punishment of the Amalekites has been long delayed (see Exod. 17:16; Num. 24:20; Deut. 20:16-18;

Josh. 6:17-21). Now, however, their cup of iniquity is full and Israel is to be God's instrument to execute judgment upon them.

The instructions from the Lord come at a most opportune time. Saul and the people have been engaged in war with their numerous enemies for a protracted period of time. Many of Israel's bravest men have fallen in battle and Saul has found it continuously necessary to conscript new soldiers into his army (see 1 Sam. 14:52). During these wars when the armies of Israel have been engaged in battle on either their eastern or western flanks, the Amalekites, wily nomads of the Negev (see Num. 13:29), have crossed Israel's southern border and plundered and pillaged the defenseless towns and villages. The command from the *LORD of hosts* to annihilate them will bring welcome relief from these incursions.

Everything the Amalekites have is to be under a *herem*, or "ban,"[4] and is to be devoted to destruction (see Lev. 27:29; Deut. 13:17). The entire campaign will necessitate that Saul have a tight hold on the situation. The people must be instructed in the purpose of their mission before the march is begun. Only those who are prepared to do as the Lord has commanded need accompany him.[5]

Saul acts with all the authority vested in him and he and his men achieve a significant victory. Saul, however, disobeys the Lord's command. He spares Agag and does not restrain the people from taking the spoils of war (15:8,9). Then, to commemorate his victory, he sets up a monument in Carmel, seven miles south of Hebron. And with all the vanity of a conquering hero, he takes Agag with him to parade him before the people at celebrations which are to be held at Gilgal. Gilgal was the place where the kingdom had been confirmed to him (see 1 Sam. 11:14), and, for reasons not stated in the text, Saul may also have felt that he needed something similar now to reinstate him in the esteem of the people.

76

Saul Repents of His Disobedience
1 Samuel 15:24-35

Unfortunately for Saul, his plans miscarry. Samuel suddenly appears. He has been down to the scene of the battle only to be told that Saul and the people have gone to Gilgal.

When Saul sees Samuel his greeting is so sweeping that he can hardly have been conscious of his offense. *Blessed are you of the LORD!* he exclaims. *I have carried out the command of the LORD* (15:13). He is totally unprepared for the prophet's reply. *What then is this bleating of the sheep in my ears? And how do you explain the lowing of the cattle which I hear?* [The evidence of my senses gives the lie to your words of assurance] (15:14).

Saul is now like a disobedient child caught with his hand in the cookie jar. His immediate response is to blame the people for his actions. He says in effect, *They made me do it. They have brought the sheep and oxen to sacrifice to the LORD your God* (15:15; see 15:9).[6]

But Saul's reasoning is as faulty as his conduct. Like the comic hero who concluded that "If it's good for General Bull Moose, it's good for the country," Saul's actions imply that "If it's good for me, it'll be good for God, too."

God, however, does not view Saul's disobedience as lightly as he does. He looks upon the heart and sees that Saul has usurped the position which He alone should occupy. Through his disobedience Saul has shown his contempt for the theocracy.[7] He is unfit to lead God's people. God's attitude toward Saul's conduct is ably expressed by Samuel: *To obey is better than sacrifice, and to hearken than the fat of rams. For rebellion [self-will] is as the sin of divination, and stubbornness is as iniquity and idolatry* (15:22,23).

Samuel knows only too well the fallacy of believing that if one follows the *general* will of God he can avoid the *specifics*. He knows too that God cannot be placated with sacrifices when a person's heart is manifestly in rebellion against His will.

77

Because you have rejected the word of the LORD, Samuel states emphatically, *He has also rejected you from being king* (15:23). Previously Saul's dynasty had been set aside (see 1 Sam. 13:13,14); now Saul himself is rejected.

This is a serious blow for Saul. He so desperately wants approval. Samuel's words now seem to place beyond his reach the very thing he desires most. Too late he expresses his willingness to change (15:24). Unfortunately for him, his belated repentance brings no remission of the sentence. He pleads with Samuel to accompany him to the place of sacrifice, but to no avail. In contrast, Samuel has spent his life maintaining the theocracy. He has lived in submission to God's authority. He is angered that a person such as Saul should treat with contempt the high position to which he has been elected. And then to observe Saul's shallow "repentance"—brought on by the consequences of his sin rather than by the realization of his offense—is more than Samuel can tolerate.

In desperation Saul falls to his knees before Samuel. The prophet, however, turns to leave. As he does so, Saul catches hold of the hem of his clothing. Most commentators believe that Saul did this in order to detain the prophet. This certainly is possible. Some recently discovered tablets at Mari on the west bank of the Euphrates River indicate, however, that at least in Akkadian times to hold the hem of a person's garment was a sign of submission and loyalty. If this symbolic gesture is indicative of Saul's action, then perhaps he finally realized that submission to Samuel's God, and loyalty to Him, constituted the wisest course of action. Unfortunately for Saul, his desire for reform is too late. Samuel's clothing tears in his hands, providing the prophet with another opportunity to reinforce God's decree. *The LORD*, he says, *has torn the kingdom from you this day* (15:28).

Realizing that God's sentence is final, Saul pleads with Samuel. *I have sinned;* he says, *yet honor me now before the*

*elders of my people and before Israel, and return with me
that I may worship your God* (15:30).

Samuel is unwilling to make Saul grovel, so he accedes
to his request and the celebrations continue. But for Saul,
dreams of popularity and acclaim have vanished.

Anointing of Saul's Successor
1 Samuel 16:1-23

Samuel, of course, leaves Gilgal and returns to Ramah.
There the Lord appears to him and instructs him to go to
Bethlehem and anoint one of the sons of Jesse to be king
over His people.

Samuel obeys. One by one Jesse's sons are brought before him. When he sees Eliab he thinks, *Surely the LORD'S
anointed is before me* (1 Sam. 16:6). The Lord, however,
rebukes him and His words to Samuel on this occasion
highlight His reason for rejecting Saul (who was outwardly
impressive and externally oriented) and selecting David
(who was spiritually in tune with His will and internally
motivated). *Do not look at his appearance or at his height,
for I do not see as man sees. For man looks at the outward
appearance, but the LORD looks at the heart.*

When all of Jesse's sons have passed before Samuel, all
except David (who, as the youngest, has the most menial
tasks assigned to him), Samuel asks, *Are these all your
children?* When he learns about David he requires that
Jesse send for him. A runner is sent to the hills outside
Bethlehem where David is caring for his father's sheep.
David returns home, and when he appears before the
prophet, the Lord instructs him to *Arise, [and] anoint him;
for this is he.* Samuel, as always, obeys, and the Spirit of the
Lord leaves Saul and *comes mightily upon David.*

A book on Second Samuel might consider David's obedience and how he came to be regarded as a *man after God's
own heart.* For the present we will return to Saul and probe
the reason for his disobedience.

Fear—Reason for Disobedience

The real reason for Saul's disobedience was *fear* (see 1 Sam. 15:24).

This same problem plagues us today. We too may be afraid that we will not be able to achieve our ambitions or fulfill our ideals if we submit to the will of God. As with Saul we begin to regard anything which threatens the realization of our plans as something to be feared.

Basically there are two primary types of people involved in situations such as this.

The *first are so externally oriented that they have little or no internal God-consciousness.* They may fulfill the broad intent of God's will (because this is the safest thing to do), but they never realize how far short they fall of following the specifics. As long as outward circumstances enable them to progress toward *their* goals, they are relatively content. When challenged with the disparity between their conduct and what God requires, their initial response is to deny the charge. If this fails, they will try to blame others for the predicament in which they find themselves. On those occasions when they are unable to get their own way they "repent" of their actions and exhibit some genuine "remorse." But their sorrow is seldom caused by any awareness of the gravity of their offense. They are invariably only sorry for what is happening to them, not for what they have done wrong.

We may well question, why does this happen? What causes people to act in this way?

In answering these questions it should be pointed out that people such as Saul have a deficient view of God. The Bible tells us that we should *fear* (reverence, or stand in awe of) God. When we do this our vertical relationship with the Lord brings the rest of life into conformity with the truth. And this gives us a proper perspective on reality. This "fear of the Lord" does not result in a life of cringing before a despotic deity (as we may at first be inclined to believe), but instead results in perfect *freedom* (see Matt. 11:28-30).

Unfortunately for Saul, his life was spent combating any number of improper fear-objects (the Philistines in 13:5-7,11,12; his own soldiers in 14:45; the people in 15:24; and Samuel in 15:13-31; later on, others). The tragedy is, lacking a spiritual dimension to his personality, he was never aware of how God viewed his actions. As a result he brought on himself and those associated with him the consequences of his disobedience.

The *second type of person* who finds himself involved in situations where his natural inclination is to disobey the revealed will of God *has both an external and an internal orientation.* When he is tempted to disobey, the internal dynamics of his God-consciousness come into play and cause a fear-conflict. This is what the New Testament calls the conflict between the flesh and the spirit (see Rom. 8:5). This inner tension can only be satisfactorily resolved and peace restored by submitting to the will of God.

To refuse to submit to the Lord and to follow, instead, one's own inclinations, invariably leads to either legalism or license. There is an excellent case in point in the life and experience of the renowned composer Franz Liszt. It was only natural that a person with such remarkable talents would draw about him a large number of admirers. Among these was a vast coterie of young women. At times Liszt's promiscuous ways would cause him to feel intense guilt. On one occasion he even entered a monastery and devoted himself to mortifying the flesh. When his fleshly instincts proved too strong for his spiritual commitments, he left the monastery and soon won fame again as a composer. His female companions allured him once more and the conflict with his emotions continued.

While vacillations between legalism and license are not always as pronounced as they were in the case of Franz Liszt, such an experience invariably results whenever God

81

is not held in the supreme position as Lord.[8]

In New Testament times believers were encouraged to nurture the spiritual dimension of their personalities so that they might grow toward maturity. This involved developing the potential God had given them. They were exhorted to *grow in grace*, conform more and more to the *image of Christ* (2 Pet. 3:18; see 2 Cor. 3:18), and take a delight in doing God's will (see Ps. 40:8). The starting place was in voluntarily submitting their wills to His will and allowing the Holy Spirit to remake them (conform them to the image of God's Son: Phil. 2:6,7). This involved the renewal of their minds (see Rom. 12:2; Eph. 4:23; Col. 3:10), the purifying of their affections (see Rom. 12:9; Col. 3:2; Jas. 4:1-10; 1 Pet. 1:22) and so partaking of the divine nature (see 2 Pet. 1:4) that they did the will of God from the heart (see Eph. 6:6).

This is what God has planned for us. He is willing and able to bring His plan to its glorious consummation if we will but acknowledge His sovereignty. In contrast to Saul we can triumph in every circumstance of life by following His will.

Interaction

1. Saul wanted the approval and praise of others more than anything else. He allowed his desire for self-gratification to come between him and God. What things do we desire most in life? (Riches? marriage? clothing? family? possessions? entertainment? sport? friends?) Do we allow these *things* to come between us and the Lord? How may we institute a change? What is the Bible's teaching regarding your particular situation?

2. Saul yielded to the temptation of obtaining what he wanted by disobeying God. How does James 1:12,14-16 enlarge on our understanding of Saul's situation (and ours)?

3. How would you explain a verse such as Proverbs 1:7 (or Prov. 8:13; 14:26,27; 15:33; 16:6)? Is what Saul searched for bound

up in this concept (see Prov. 22:4)? In what ways does this apply to us today?

4. Why are we prone to the extremes of legalism and license? In what ways do these tendencies manifest themselves in our lives?

5. A case study: A missionary in his early 40s, home on furlough from East Africa, visits a Christian counselor. He is concerned about his spiritual condition. "I'm facing the same problems now (hankering after material possessions, desire for illicit sex relations, etc.) that I faced 20 years ago," he says. "I thought those battles had been fought and *won* long ago." Further discussion indicates that he lives by a rigid moral code (legalism) and this is why he is so concerned over the power of his desires. While on the mission station, and busy with his work, it has been relatively easy to suppress his feelings . . . (although he also admits to occasionally indulging his fantasies, i.e., his desire for license). If you were his counselor, how would you help him? What suggestions would you make?

Footnotes

1. The *New English Bible* translates Proverbs 31:21 "two cloaks." This is done by changing the order of the letters in the word and shows a very low regard for the inspiration of the text. Other versions use "wool," or claim that Saul clothed the people of Israel "luxuriously." These latter views, while less acceptable than "warmly" are preferable to "two cloaks."

2. Note the words *"us"* and *"we"* in 1 Samuel 9:5-10.

3. *Elohim tsebhaoth* is the usual term for "Lord of hosts." In 1 Samuel 15:2 it is *Yahweh tsebhaoth.* Its usage emphasizes not only God's right to lead the armies of Israel but His unique covenant relationship with His people as well. A person such as Paul would have to be very insensitive not to realize the supreme importance of obeying such an explicit command.

4. Compare Joshua 7. The penalty for breaking the "ban" has been described in Cyril J. Barber, *God Has the Answer . . . to Your Problems* (Grand Rapids: Baker Books, 1974), pp. 93ff.

5. The large numbers that gather at Telaim (1 Sam. 15:4) indicate that Saul had not instructed the people as to the nature of their mission. Verse 19 further indicates that the people felt under no restraint and "took of the spoils" of war as the just compensation of their labor.

6. Three times in this account Saul refers to the Lord as *Samuel's* God (1 Sam. 15:15,21, 30). The repetition of this phrase indicates that Saul has no personal relationship with the One to whom he refers.

7. The term "theocracy" comes from two Greek words, *theos*, "God," and *kratein*, "to rule." It looks at God's rule over His earthly people through a local representative (i.e., Saul). Seen in this light, we can easily understand Samuel's anger at Saul's conduct and also God's rejection of him as king.

8. Saul's life was spent pursuing an improper fear-object, *license*. This does not mean that, on occasions, the pendulum did not swing in the other direction. Examples of his sudden *legalism* may be found in 1 Samuel 14:24,32-35; 19:6; 24:16-22; etc.

7
ANATOMY OF A FAILURE

1 SAMUEL 17:1-40

All of us are subject to stress. No matter how well we may plan our lives, there are times when the pressures of unforeseen circumstances threaten to overwhelm us. The proof of the reality of our Christian experience is demonstrated in the way we handle these tensions.

James Hudson Taylor, founder of the China Inland Mission (now the Overseas Missionary Fellowship), knew what it was like to face trial and misfortune, difficulty and loss. How he dealt with the internal and external pressures associated with the work of the mission is told in *Hudson Taylor's Spiritual Secret*.

One of Hudson Taylor's most trying experiences occurred during the Yangchow Riot. The British Parliament severely criticized the work of missions in China. Missionaries from the different denominations were blamed for the strained diplomatic relations. Financial support dwindled and tensions increased. Many of the missionaries were so filled with fear that their trust in the Lord began to fail. Strong leadership was needed if the work was to survive the crisis.

It was during this period of time that Hudson Taylor gave expression to one of the most important truths found in the book. He wrote "It doesn't matter, really, how great the pressure is, it only matters *where the pressure lies.*"[1] By means of his own unshakable faith in God he was able to encourage others. He believed that the external threats they were facing would either draw them closer to the Lord or drive them from Him.

Of importance to us are the experiences of two men in the Bible who faced the pressure of circumstances they could not control. These men are Saul and David. The way in which they responded to the difficulty is as instructive as it is revealing. In Saul's case the external threat did not draw him closer to the Lord. In David's experience the same pressure increased his reliance upon God. Their combined examples illustrate, first negatively and then positively, the responses of people to pressure. David illustrates for us the value of faith and how it may become a dynamic working force—a reality—in our lives.

A Difficult Situation
1 Samuel 17:1-11

Following Jonathan's success over the Philistine garrison (see 1 Sam. 15) and Saul's partial victory, the Philistines quickly regroup their forces and launch a new attack on the Israelites. They invade the south and take command of the Elah Valley. By controlling the valley they also control the approaches to the mountains of Judah. Saul and his armies face a difficult situation. Their supply routes from the west have been cut off and they must take decisive action. They leave the fortress-city of Gibeah,[2] north of Jerusalem, and assemble for battle—the Philistines on one side of the valley and the Israelites on the other.

The description which follows is most interesting. Instead of the usual battle, we read: *A champion came out from the armies of the Philistines named Goliath . . . whose height was six cubits and a span.[3] And he had a bronze helmet on his head, and he was clothed with scale armor which weighed 5,000 shekels of bronze. He also had bronze shin guards on his legs and a bronze javelin slung between his shoulders. And the shaft of his spear was like a weaver's beam, and the head of his spear weighed six hundred shekels of iron; and his shieldbearer went before him.[4] And he stood and shouted to the ranks of Israel, and said to them, 'Why do you come out to draw up in battle array? Am I not a Philistine and you the servants of Saul? Choose a man for yourselves and let him come down to me. If he is able to fight with me and kill me, then we [the Philistines] will become your servants; but if I prevail against him and kill him, then you shall become our servants and serve us'* (17:4-9).

A close look at the passage shows that Goliath is not only being arrogant and boastful, he is also proposing a new kind of warfare.[5] He is challenging the Israelites to send a representative who will engage him in mortal combat. The fate of both nations will hinge on the outcome of the contest.

This incident is very revealing. It shows us that even in those early days armies in the Near East felt keenly the loss of their fighting men. Some armies, therefore, chose a champion to duel with a representative of the opposing army. The fate of both sides would rest entirely on the outcome of the duel.

Evidence of this phenomenon has been supplied by archaeologists who have unearthed an orthostat from the palace of Kapara at Tell Halaf. This stone carving shows two men, each holding the other's hair in his left hand and short swords in their right hands, dueling. In addition, extant texts from different countries in the ancient Near Eastern world parallel the conditions of the contest Goliath laid down. There was first the challenge followed by negotiation and the method of combat. All of this suggests that combat between representatives of two opposing armies was quite common. It also explains why, on the death of Goliath, the Philistines turned and fled. They knew they had lost!

Saul's Response to Pressure

When Goliath threw down the gauntlet before the armies of Israel, no one accepted his challenge. The question naturally arises, "Why didn't Saul accept Goliath's challenge?" He was the most likely person to fight against him. He was the most qualified by office, size and experience. The truth of the matter is that Saul was no longer fit to lead the armies of the Lord. The Spirit of God had departed from him (see 1 Sam. 16:14) and he had lost the divine enabling which formerly he enjoyed.

Saul's orientation had always been external. In this instance he sized up the situation, compared his size with the giant's, his armor and weapons with the Philistine's, and concluded that he was unequal to the task. Someone else might take on Goliath but not he.

It is of interest for us to notice that in this time of crisis Saul did *not* turn to the Lord and place his confidence in Him. To be sure, God had reproved Saul in the past and had also told him that his kingdom was to be taken from him (see 1 Sam. 15:28), but this did not prevent Saul from repenting of his sin and seeking the Lord. The gates of heaven were not shut against him and God would assuredly have heard his prayer. But Saul never considered entreating God's favor, for the Lord was *not* the object of his faith. As a result he had no inward stability and nothing to strengthen him during this crisis.

In the face of the growing tension, Saul feels the need for action. He turns to his men and promises to make the man who kills Goliath rich beyond compare. He will also make him his son-in-law, give him an honored place in his palace, and exempt his father's house from taxes (1 Sam. 17:25). By offering this "bribe," Saul takes the eyes of his followers off his own failure as a leader and fixes them on the external rewards he is offering them. (If the contender loses the contest, the Israelites will, of course, become the subjects of the Philistines. They will, however, be allowed to return to their farms and be subject to extra taxation each year. And, Saul by promising to be loyal to the Philistines, will probably be retained in office as a vassal.) It's a neat plan with little risk attached to it.

David's Reliance on God
1 Samuel 17:12-40

For nearly six weeks, morning and evening, Goliath has proudly shouted out his challenge (17:16). One morning, apparently quite by accident, as Goliath is upbraiding the armies of Israel, a young shepherd boy named David enters the camp. He is bringing food to his brothers (17:17-19). The war cry of the Israelites (17:20), which he had only recently heard, has suddenly become muted as the men of Israel listen in fear to the challenge of the giant from Gath (17:24).

In contrast to his fellow countrymen, however, David feels no fear. He is not overawed by the size of the Philistine. He hears Goliath's blasphemous challenge and wonders why no one has met him in open combat. His internal orientation places the whole situation in its proper perspective. He sees clearly the spiritual issues involved. Anyone who defies *the armies of the living God* (17:10,36) is denouncing the theocracy of which God is the Head. Goliath is, in effect, taunting God. He is issuing his challenge to the Almighty. David knows that on an earlier occasion Pharaoh, king of Egypt, did the same thing (see Exod. 5:2). The result to Pharaoh was the death of the firstborn and the destruction of his armies (Exod. 12:29; 14:26-28). Can Goliath expect to fare any better?

David lets it be known that he will accept the Philistine's challenge and is brought before Saul. His words are full of assurance: *Let no man's heart fail on account of him; your servant will go and fight with this Philistine* (17:32). In contrast to Saul and the armies of Israel, David is confident. Saul's ineptitude has weakened the faith and lowered the morale of his men. David, on the other hand, has his confidence in the Lord and this gives him confidence in himself.

Saul tries to dissuade David from accepting Goliath's challenge. He points out that David is a mere shepherd boy who has never known the brunt of battle. He also contrasts his experience to Goliath's and points out that Goliath has been a warrior from his youth. Saul, however, is motivated solely by external considerations and measures events and circumstances by a carnal standard. His assessment of the situation leaves God out!

When he realizes that he cannot dissuade David from accepting the giant's challenge, Saul offers the young shepherd the use of his armor. Outwardly this appears to be a magnanimous gesture. A coat of mail had to be carefully forged, was very costly, and few in Israel possessed one. Inwardly, however, Saul is motivated by fear. He knows David is taking his place and he wants to do whatever he can to help him. Then, if David is successful, he can claim some of the credit.

When David tries on the armor he finds that it impedes his movements and decides to go against Goliath without it. The Lord gives him a great victory and the Israelites chase their enemies all the way to the border towns of Philistia.

Fear-Object or Faith-Object?

But we may well ask, What does this have to do with us?

As we assess the situation we find that Saul was weak because he had an improper fear-object. He stood in awe of Goliath because of the giant's greater height and superior weapons. His fear caused him to lose perspective and completely distorted his view of reality. He saw only Goliath's might and, by comparison, his own impotence.

Saul's fear of Goliath incapacitated him as a leader. His spirit of apprehension infected his men and they lost their confidence. In this state they dared not accept the giant's challenge. That is why their early battle cry (17:20)—much like a cheerleader's at a football game when their team is losing—was so easily silenced (17:24).

Saul and his men made the mistake of attributing almightiness to Goliath. They were weak because they lacked a proper faith-object. They needed the spiritual insight David possessed. He had internal principles to guide him and recognized at once the real character of Goliath's challenge. From his previous experience of God's faithfulness he knew that God would deliver the Philistine into his hands as easily as He had him master the lion and bear. This confidence in the Lord gave him confidence in himself. He could, therefore, face the giant without fear.

Faith Overcomes Difficult Situations

The apostle John tells us that faith is the principle which enables us to overcome the difficulties of life (see 1 John 5:4). True faith involves a commitment of ourselves to the Lord. Our confidence must be in Him and in no one else. Those who are externally oriented—those whose view of reality is determined solely by their senses—are particularly prone to failure. They lack inner stability and desperately need the kind of strengthening which can come only from placing their confidence in the Lord. Unfortunately, many externally-oriented people seek for security in alliances and different kinds of relationships. As time goes by they begin to doubt those whom they have admitted to their confidence and sooner or later their own fears undermine and finally destroy their relationships.

The internally oriented, on the other hand, have their trust in the Lord and find that the trials and difficulties of life drive them closer to Him. They are not dependent on people who may betray their confidence or let them down. And because of the spiritual dynamic God imparts to them, they are able to triumph over every circumstance (see Rom. 8:37).

Several years ago a young woman came to her pastor for counseling. Her husband had died and the difficulties associated with the rearing of her family seemed to overwhelm her. Her pastor showed her from the Word how she could lay her problems on Christ and have Him bear her burdens (see 1 Pet. 5:7). As the conversation progressed, she came to see that she had been relying on her own strength instead of availing herself of His resources. From that hour the Lord Jesus became the object of her trust. As each new difficulty arose she drew closer to Him and, in a way that was easily discernable to those about her, she was able to rise above the inner trials and outward pressures of life.

In a southern city a Christian businessman faced financial difficulties which he was powerless to control. One night, overwhelmed by all that pressed in upon him, he surrendered himself and his business to the Lord. He later acknowledged that he had been kept from trusting the Lord because he had an incorrect view of who God was. He looked upon Him solely as a punitive deity, not as a loving Father. With this new outlook this Christian businessman enjoyed a new confidence. He knew that he was the object of his Father's love and care. The things he formerly could not do on his own, God was now able to accomplish through him.

A change in the object of our faith will *not* remove the external pressures from our lives but will enable us to cope with them. As with David, we can triumph over the circumstances which threaten us.

Interaction

1. Saul's whole approach to life was on the basis of external criteria. To him, reality consisted of the things he could identify with his senses. In what ways did this handicap him in handling the crisis described in verses 4-11? How did it distort the true reality?

2. In what subtle ways did Saul's fear of the Philistine threat demoralize his men? How did he try to compensate for this? Why did he fail?

3. David had the proper faith-object—the Lord. Why did this give him confidence? Why was David able to succeed where Saul failed?

Proper faith-object: God
Result: Strength, confidence

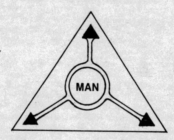

Improper faith-object: Circumstances—Goliath
Result: Weakness, feeling of inadequacy, lack of confidence, cowardice

Improper faith-object: Things—armor, spear, etc.
Result: Obscuring of the real issues, leaving God out, relying on own resources

4. Saul could have turned to the Lord in repentance and faith, but he did not. God's previous rebukes (see 1 Sam. 13:13,14; 15:26,28) left him feeling that God was like his own father. Why was this a wrong view of God? What could have corrected this? How may our own view of God be conditioned by our

parents? What are we doing to insure that we create a proper God-consciousness in our children?

5. Learning to have a proper faith-object takes time. It involves growth (see 2 Pet. 3:18). In what area of your life are you now learning to trust God implicitly?

Footnotes

1. Howard and Geraldine Taylor, *Hudson Taylor's Spiritual Secret* (Chicago: Moody, n.d.), p. 152. Italics in the original.

2. During 1922-23 William F. Albright excavated Gibeah. He found Saul's "palace" to be of simple design and more like a fortress than a lavish residence. See his books, *From the Stone Age to Christianity* (Garden City: Doubleday, 1957), p. 224; and *Archaeology of Palestine* (London: Penguin Books, 1954), pp. 120-22.

3. A cubit was approximately 18 inches. A span would represent about 9-12 inches. This would make Goliath approximately 10 feet tall. His coat of mail alone weighed about 150 pounds and made him virtually impregnable. His weapons were sufficient to make anyone cringe with fear. The head of his javelin weighed 20 pounds and could pierce through normal armor. He was a most formidable adversary!

4. The Hebrew *tsinnah* refers to a large shield which was used to protect the whole body.

5. Duels of this nature are found in ancient literature. Examples may be found in the story of Sohrab and Rustum, popularized by Matthew Arnold; the challenge of Paris to Menelaus, told by Homer in his *Iliad*; and the fight of Sinuhe, the Egyptian, with a man of Retenu (*Ancient Near Eastern Texts*, p. 20). These provide illustrations of this phenomenon. See also Roland de Vaux, *The Bible and the Ancient Near East* (Garden City, NY: Doubleday, 1971), pp. 122-135.

6. An orthostat is a large stone slab riveting the lower part of a cella or principle enclosed chamber. Orthostats were frequently grouped together and have been found by archaeologists who have unearthed the temples of antiquity. The orthostat referred to in this chapter may be seen in the Berlin Museum. These orthostats shed light on passages such as 2 Samuel 2:12,17; 21:18,19; 1 Chronicles 11:23.

THE KEY TO
UNCOMPLICATED LIVING

1 SAMUEL 17:25-58

What is the difference between faith and presumption?
How may a person know that his idealism is God-inspired
and not man-directed? By what means does faith in spiritual realities help us overcome the pressures of life?

These questions find their answer in David, a man after
God's own heart. For nearly six weeks the Israelites have
listened to the taunts and ridicule of Goliath. Twice a day
he challenged them to send a representative to fight with
him. His words produced only dismay in the hearts of the
Israelites. Cowardice is something they share in common.
They are incapable of handling this kind of threat. To a
man, they prefer humiliation to hand-to-hand combat.

Their situation was similar to circumstances which face
each one of us. There are times in our lives when we are
threatened by external forces. When there is a change in
"the man at the top," for example, employees experience

a feeling of insecurity. The thwarting of a long-cherished plan may cause us to experience an immediate fear of failure. Some bad news, or the passing of a loved one, threatens to push the bottom out of our world. These and many other external threats may leave us in the same condition as Saul and the men of his army—deprived of power and inwardly depressed.

Fortunately for us, God has shown us how to handle problems of this nature. In the attitude of David He has given us an illustration of how we, too, may cope with the pressures which face us.

A Matter of Confidence
1 Samuel 17:25

As David approaches the camp of the Israelites on that eventful morning, he is surprised to hear Goliath's blasphemous challenge. He is also astonished to find that no one has accepted the giant's invitation. Such a flagrant rejection of Israel's theocratic administration by the Philistine cannot go unpunished. As Matthew Henry has shown, the effrontery offered them reflects upon the living God Himself. God is obligated to defend His honor. Goliath, though he did not know it, was as good as dead.[1]

As David mingles with the soldiers, he tries to encourage them by sharing with them his confidence in the Lord. One of them, who feels keenly the humiliation of the Israelites, rebukes David. *Have you seen this man?* he asks. Obviously he implies that if David had seen Goliath he would not speak in such a precocious way. His rebuff releases an avalanche of criticism. Another soldier who also lacks the perception of faith which David possesses, remarks: *He [Goliath] is coming up to defy Israel.* By implication he infers that this is a national, not a religious, matter. His answer shows that he sees no relationship between the nation and God. And a third comments wistfully, *The king will enrich the man who kills Goliath with great riches and will give him his daughter and exempt his father's house from taxation and public service* (17:25).

Confidence Before the Soldiers
1 Samuel 17:26-30

David is not discouraged by these rebukes. He uses Saul's inducements to encourage the men to action: *What will be done for the man who kills this Philistine, and takes away the reproach from Israel?* he asks one group. Then he provides the assurance of faith. *For who is this uncircumcised Philistine, that he should taunt the armies of the living God* (17:26)?

David obviously evaluates the situation from the sure foundation of confidence in the Lord. He finds, however, that neither the promise of wealth and honor nor the stabilizing effect of faith is sufficient to persuade anyone to expose himself to the danger of single combat with Goliath. So fearful have the men become that they miss the point of what David is saying.

It is at this juncture that the embarrassment becomes more than Eliab, David's oldest brother, can bear. He feels humiliated because his youngest brother—too young to take up arms himself—presumes to encourage the fighting men of Israel. He censures David with words designed to soothe his own hurt feelings and transfer some of the frustration he feels to his brother. He accuses David of careless indifference to his own responsibilities (caring for the sheep) and of meddling in the affairs of others.

The response of Eliab and the soldiers is typical of the experience of the fearful. Fear blinds the eye and debilitates the will. So fearful of Goliath are they that they cannot see the issues clearly. When encouragement comes they are too preoccupied with their own feelings to be strengthened by it. Fear makes them insensitive to all David is saying. As Shakespeare pointed out in *Richard III*, "You cannot reason with a man who is full of dread."

Furthermore, fear of Goliath has led to smoldering resentment. But this anger can find no outlet; it is bottled up like soda water. When David comes to the camp with his words of encouragement, the cap pops off and the pent-up emotions of the men (and particularly Eliab) are released. The result is the cruel taunting and unjust criticism which we read in the text.

David's response to Eliab is most instructive. He avoids becoming embroiled in an illogical debate. He merely says: *What have I done now? Was it not just a word [a question]?* (17:29). He could have used reason to vindicate his point of view. Instead of carrying on the argument which Eliab had begun, his reply disarms his brother's anger (see Prov. 15:1; 16:32; Jas. 1:19,20,26). He then turns away from Eliab and by so doing avoids further discussion.

Confidence Before Saul
1 Samuel 17:31-39

It is possible that by this time David, having found no one to represent the armies of Israel and defend the honor of the Lord, volunteers to accept Goliath's challenge. We do know that before long he is brought before Saul. His implicit trust in God gives him inward security and a balanced self-confidence. In response to Saul's inquiry David says: *Let no man's heart fail on account of him [Goliath]. Your servant will go and fight with this Philistine* (17:32). In this offer to pick up the gauntlet Goliath threw down, David's strong internal motivation is revealed.

Saul, so accustomed to viewing situations externally, immediately tries to dissuade David. He contrasts his age and experience with that of the challenger from Gath: *You are not able to go and fight against this Philistine,* he says, *for you are but a youth while he has been a warrior from his youth* (17:33).

In the same tactful way that David handled Eliab's outburst with meekness,[2] he now explains to Saul the reason for his faith. He, too, has experience to draw on. As a shepherd he previously fought single-handed with a lion and a bear. His courage matches his confidence: *The LORD who delivered me from the paw of the lion and the paw of the bear, He will deliver me from the hand of this Philistine* (17:36).

The contrast between Saul and David is obvious. Saul, on the one hand, measures everything by a carnal standard and knows nothing of the faith which moves mountains. David, on the other hand, is an example of a human being linked with the invisible God. His strength is derived from inner resources and his trust in the Lord gives him confidence in himself. Remembrance of God's past deliverances gives him assurance as he faces the present crisis. His faith displaces all fear.

As David stands before Saul, the king is dubious. He wonders if he should risk the fortunes of the nation on a youth. However, as David explains God's part, Saul becomes convinced of the young shepherd's sincerity and reliance upon the Lord. Perhaps he remembers the early days of his own reign when the Lord was with him. He admires David's self-confidence and finally agrees to the contest. Realizing that David is ill-equipped, Saul offers him the use of his weapons and armor. David tries on the armor, but, like a child trying on his father's coat, he finds that it is several sizes too big for him. It only hinders his movements. David, therefore, lays Saul's equipment aside and, descending into the *wadi*,[3] advances to meet Goliath.

Confidence Before Goliath
1 Samuel 17:40-58

In place of Saul's weapons David selects five stones from a small stream which flows through the valley. With these in his pouch he moves toward the Philistine.

The type of sling[4] which David used in fighting Goliath is used by shepherds in eastern lands to this day. Unlike a western slingshot, it is made out of two leather thongs with a pad in the middle. The one thong is fastened around the wrist while the other is held in the hand. A stone is placed in the pad and the sling is then whirled around the head. The stone becomes dislodged as the one thong is released. Those who have observed Bedouin children using slings know something of the accuracy with which they can throw a stone.

On seeing David approach, Goliath begins to mock him. He had expected a *man* to come and fight against him, not a boy. David isn't even equipped with the right weapons. Goliath curses David by his gods and threatens to flay his body so that birds and animals may feast on it.

This kind of taunting was to be expected. It was all part of the "psychological warfare" of the day, and was designed to discourage the opponent. It was something which the people in eastern lands were most adept at, and similar exchanges may be found in the classical literature of the Greeks and Romans.[5]

For Goliath's benefit David clarifies the issues: *You come to me with a sword, a spear, and a javelin, but I come to you in the name of the LORD of hosts, the God of the armies of Israel, whom you have taunted. This day the LORD will deliver you up into my hands, and I will strike you down and remove your head from you. And I will give the dead bodies of the army of the Philistines this day to the birds of the sky and the wild beasts of the earth, that all the earth may know that there is a God in Israel, and that all this assembly may know that the LORD does not deliver by sword or by spear; for the battle is the LORD's and He will give you into our hands* (17:45-47).

The picture conjured up before our minds by this exchange is vivid and revealing. In contrast to Goliath's vainglorious pride there is David's humble reliance upon the Lord—a reliance which would result in putting an army to flight (see Heb. 11:34; compare Deut. 32:30).

100

Goliath is so angered by this expression of confidence that he rises to his feet and advances toward David. David runs to meet the giant, eager to prove the truth of his words. As he moves forward he puts his hand into his bag and takes from it a stone. He inserts it into his sling, and whirling it around his head, he releases the one end so that the smooth stone flies out of the free end. The stone strikes the Philistine on his forehead causing him to fall to the ground. A man of lesser faith than David's might have been too nervous to take proper aim. Undisturbed by the fear of failure, David hits the mark—Goliath's forehead—the only unprotected part of his person. Then, before the giant can regain his senses, David runs to him and, drawing his sword from its sheath, cuts off Goliath's head. The whole encounter takes no more than a few seconds.

The Philistines watch this brief duel from their side of the valley in disbelief. When they realize what has happened, they flee. The men of Israel pursue them to the border towns of Gath and Ekron, and the invaders suffer a defeat.

David is given a position in the army of Saul (see 1 Sam. 18:2) and places the spoils of war in his tent.[6]

The Source of David's Confidence

Several practical lessons emerge from this incident. They center in the way in which we face external pressures. We all encounter events which threaten us and disturb our tranquility. What principles, therefore, may we learn from David's example which will give us insights into our own problems?

First, *David succeeded because of his unshakable confidence in God's faithfulness.* In contrast to Saul, he was well-grounded in the theology of his day and possessed a strong personal faith. This knowledge gave him perspective on the situation and placed him in touch with reality. As a result he had a different outlook to the king's. He did not feel threatened. Even Saul's negative assessment of the

101

situation did not cause him to lose heart. His inner orientation equipped him to cope with pressure. He realized that his life was in God's hands. And inasmuch as God is sovereign, what did he have to fear?

This confidence in God also gave David a new set of values. He did not agree to duel with Goliath because he wanted riches or power or prestige. He was interested in God's honor alone. He knew that Goliath had insulted the Lord and defied the covenant-keeping "Suzerain" of Israel. David accepted Goliath's challenge because he wanted to vindicate the One whom he trusted. His inner devotion to the Lord was greater than his desire for material gain.

Second, *David's confidence was also based upon past experience.* In spite of his youthfulness, he had experienced God's providential undertaking in the past. The incidents with a lion and a bear had given him such assurance in God's protective care that he realized he could trust the Lord in all the circumstances of his life.

Saul, on the other hand, was like those people who never learn from the intervention of the Lord in their lives. Earlier in his experience God had given him a remarkable victory (see 1 Sam. 11:6-11), but instead of learning to trust the Lord, he acted presumptuously (1 Sam. 13:5-10) and relied upon himself. He collapsed before outward pressure because he had no inner principles to guide him. He was never truly convinced of God's involvement in his life for any length of time.

David faced external threats with inner confidence. He was fortified against external peril by the conscious knowledge that God was working behind the scenes on his behalf. His faith sustained him as he faced each new situation. In this respect he provides an important antidote to those who think that *luck* and their own ability are the only things that count.

This matter of trust is vitally important. It is as inconsistent for us *not* to trust the Lord as it is for us to allow a mechanic to work on a car and then refuse to allow him to take a nail from the tire. David shows that we should learn from our past experiences so that in times of difficulty we may trust the Lord implicitly.

Third, *David's confidence was based upon spiritual principles.* He evaluated Goliath's challenge in the light of his doctrinal commitments and concluded that the giant was guilty of blasphemy (17:45). Unlike those whose doctrine is purely theoretical, David applied his beliefs to the nitty-gritty of life. To him God was very real. He submitted to His claims and trusted in His power. As a result, he took the initiative and did not have to wait for outward pressure to force him to take action.

All of us are confronted with pressures too great for us, that often weigh us down. David's trust in God helped him overcome the trials and difficulties he faced. We face the danger of becoming overawed by the crisis[7] and forget to draw upon the resources of God. God does not expect us to succumb to difficulties, but allows them to enter our lives in order that we may triumph over them.

Interaction

1. In what ways do David's actions in this chapter illustrate the difference between faith and presumption? What may we learn from him?

2. David's tact is much in evidence with (a) the soldiers, (b) Eliab, and (c) Saul. So was his self-assertiveness. How was he able to balance these characteristics? In what ways may we apply the principles of his life to our situation?

3. Discuss the statement, "Fear makes cowards of us all," first, in relation to Saul and his men; and then in relation to us and our work for the Lord.

4. Saul and David faced the same external threat. What brought David to the fore in this crisis? Why was he successful? How may principles from this chapter be applied to the church today (see 1 Cor. 11:19)?

5. Why do you think David was described as "a man after God's own heart"?

Footnotes

1. It is a very dangerous thing to challenge or defy God, or to hold in contempt His covenant with His people. Pharaoh tried it (see Exod. 5:2) and brought on himself and his people the famous plagues of Egypt. Belshazzar mocked God in his impious and sacrilegious feast, and died (see Dan. 5:2-30).

2. The word *meek* does not mean "weak," as so many suppose, but infers the ability a person possesses to bridle his strength.

3. A rocky watercourse which is invariably dry except during rainy seasons. There is a good description of this locality in Edersheim's *Bible History*, vol. 4, pp. 87f.

4. See Yigael Yadin, *The Art of Warfare in Biblical Lands* (New York: McGraw-Hill, 1963), vol. 2; pp. 265-67,364.

5. See Homer, *The Iliad*, vol. 3, 340ff.; vol. 7, 206; etc.; Livy, I, 23.

6. Some expositors amend the text of 1 Samuel 17:54. In place of *be'oholo*, "his tent," they prefer *be'oholi* and take the final "*i*" to refer to the "tent of Yahweh." This is done on the assumption that in 21:8,9 Goliath's sword is found at Nob. There is nothing, however, to contradict the view that David was given a tent of his own in the army of Saul (1 Sam. 18:2) and that David placed Goliath's sword first in his own tent and then later transferred it to the tabernacle at Nob.

7. When this happens we inevitably capitulate to an improper fear-object. We attribute certain characteristics to the person or event—such as *almightiness* and *impendency* (i.e., the fear of imminent danger). This tends to eclipse our God-ward relationship. For a discussion of this concept see Robert E. Morosco's article on the "Theological Implications of Fear," *Journal of Psychology and Theology*, vol. 1 (April, 1973), pp. 43-50.

A LEGACY OF HATE

1 SAMUEL 18:6-30; 19:11-24

Anger is an emotion we all share, even though we express it in different ways. Most of us find "socially acceptable" methods of concealing anger, such as repressing or denying it. However, when anger is not treated honestly and objectively it is channeled into a kind of emotional reservoir of slush. In time, this slush accumulates and builds up pressure within us. When the pressure becomes too great for us to handle, it bursts through the barriers of social restraint. These outbursts—loss of temper—are invariably followed by an easing of the internal pressure. We may even be sorry for what we have said (or done) and promise that it will never happen again. We may excuse ourselves by saying, "I don't know what happened to me. I suddenly found myself saying (or doing) things I never dreamed I would ever say (or do)." But with the passing of time, denied anger begins to build up once more.

Exactly what causes us to develop this slush will vary with each individual. There are three primary causes of anger common to all of us. There is (1) the *frustration* we feel when things do not go according to our plan; (2) the *humiliation* we suffer when people look down on us; and (3) the resentment we experience when we face the *rejection* of others. Saul illustrates what happens when perverted emotions begin to poison our attitudes, distort our sense of reality and upset our interpersonal relations.

Anger, the Result of Pressure
1 Samuel 18:1-11

We saw an outpouring of anger in Saul's life first when he slaughtered the oxen and sent their dismembered parts throughout the land. This was a direct result of Saul's feeling of frustration because he did not know what to do now that he was king.

On another occasion Saul threatened to execute Jonathan after Jonathan unwittingly disobeyed Saul's ban and ate honey. This irrational outpouring of emotional slush can also be traced to the frustration Saul experienced through his imagined rejection and self-imposed inactivity.

Now we find that pressure is again building up within Saul. Even though he is the most qualified man in Israel to accept Goliath's challenge, Saul turns the task over to a young shepherd boy, David. David achieves the victory Saul should have won and, for the time being, the pressure is alleviated.

Following the duel Saul appoints David to his regular army and David continues to distinguish himself in the field of battle. He is sent out on several important missions and always meets with success. In the course of time *Saul sets him over the men of war* (18:5) and due partly to David's physical prowess, courage and personality, the young commander captures the hearts of the people.

On returning to Israel after a particularly successful campaign against the Philistines, the army is met by a group of women who have gathered to welcome home the conquering heroes. One of the local poets has evidently composed a ballad which puts Saul and David in an unfortunate contrast. The song, *Saul has slain his thousands and David his ten thousands,* (18:7) which was so pleasing to the young girls, is nevertheless displeasing to the king (18:8,9). It accords David the acclaim Saul had always wanted and from that day on he *eyes* David with suspicion.[1]

But why does this song of the women affect Saul adversely? What would cause him to react in such frenzy in his house? Was he aware that the same Power which had previously favored him is now resting on David?

It should be remembered that in the preceding chapter Saul did not accept Goliath's challenge. Now, when he hears David's virtues extolled, his long-smoldering anger is aroused. His hurt pride—his guilt because he has abdicated his position and responsibility, and loss of self-esteem—humiliation—add pressure to the anger-producing machinery of his personality. The results are the production of a deep and agonizing depression (an *evil spirit from the Lord*), an uncontrolled expression of his resentment (*he raves[2] in the midst of his house*), and the overflowing of the reservoir of slush in a hostile action (he throws his spear at David intending to *strike him [and pin him to] the wall)* (18:10,11). David, of course, escapes and this serves only to increase Saul's fear.[3] The king becomes dominated with the desire to dispose of so threatening a rival (18:13). He now intends to have David killed in combat.

So successful is David in all that he does that Saul's fear turns to dread! Even his wishes are frustrated; and with no outlet for his emotions—alternating now between anger and fear—his pent-up hostilities are fed back into his pool of slush.

Anger Expressed in Secret Vengeance
1 Samuel 18:12-30

As time passes the pressure of slush continues to grow.

107

Saul is no longer able to handle his emotional anger in an acceptable way. His thoughts turn to vengeance. His plans are calculated and vindictive. Disguising his anger behind the mask of congeniality, he promises David his eldest daughter[4] in marriage if he will *be a valiant man . . . and fight the LORD'S battles* (18:17). He hopes that David will engage in reckless acts of daring and become a casualty of war. But when the wedding day dawns, Merab, Saul's daughter, is given to someone else.

David, naturally, was deeply disappointed at this unhappy turn of events. His disappointment, however, does not cause him to lose faith in God's sovereignty or act irresponsibly. He continues to behave himself wisely, unaware that his godly behavior and continued military success are the cause of Saul's mounting frustration.

Again Saul tries to cause David to *fall by the hand of the Philistines* (18:21). This time he offers David the hand of his younger daughter. Whether Saul also felt the need (at least outwardly) to placate David for having given Merab to another, we will never know. We do know that his seemingly generous offer serves only as a cloak to hide his murderous intention. He asks as a dowry 100 foreskins of the Philistines. David more than fulfills Saul's requirements (18:27), and Michal is given him in marriage. Now, however, Saul fears David even more, and he becomes *David's enemy continually* (18:29).

One cannot help but wonder what Saul would have done had David not conducted himself in such an exemplary manner. Saul obviously is troubled by David because he has nothing to react to. David gives him no cause for offense (compare Rom. 12:18; 1 Thess. 5:22). Saul's anger, therefore, feeds itself and becomes more and more explosive.

Saul's Anger Explodes into Violence
1 Samuel 19:1-17

Perverted anger or slush sometimes becomes more overt

than subtle; and this is what happened in Saul's experience. In place of his schemes Saul now speaks only to Jonathan and his servants. He wants *them to put David to death* (19:1).

Jonathan intercedes for David. As he talks openly and honestly about Saul's malicious intentions, the king's anger temporarily dissipates. The truth produces a healing effect on his emotions and he suddenly reverses his position. *As the LORD lives*, he exclaims, *David shall not be put to death* (19:6).

The open expression of our emotions may take the explosive force away from our anger, but it does not deal with the root cause of the problem. The anger is no longer "combustible," but it still is present. Saul (as with others who talk freely about their feelings) now feels some temporary relief. His obsession is no longer as pronounced as before. He is more rational and exhibits a willingness to listen to reason. Unfortunately, his apparently benign disposition is only temporary. In time, the inward pressure will increase and his anger will erupt with little provocation.

When David returns from another successful war against the Philistines, Saul suffers from a recurrence of his former depression (19:8-10). David attempts to soothe his feelings but to no avail. Saul is now beyond help. As David plays his harp, the king again throws his spear at David. David accepts the fact that his life is in danger and escapes to his home. During the night Michal becomes aware of her father's malicious intentions. She may have seen soldiers in front of their home and detected them at the rear as well. She realizes that her father's malignant hatred will not be satisfied until David is dead. She therefore helps David escape by lowering him through a window (19:11-17).

Saul's future actions and decisions will find him in increased opposition to the obvious will of God[5] (see 1 Sam. 20). He will pursue David with relentless vigor only to find that David will slip through his fingers again and again. His personality will become so poisoned by hate that nothing will be able to stop him from destroying those who appear to oppose his will.

Saul's bitterness will reach a new nadir when he hears that David has camped at Hareth on the edge of the mountain chain of Hebron. He will assemble an army and, before marching south, will cajole those in his presence (see 1 Sam. 22:7,8). The rebuke will goad Doeg, the chief of his herdsmen, into telling the king of an event which he witnessed at Nob (see 1 Sam. 21:1-9). In fleeing from Saul, David visited the priests at Nob and obtained food and Goliath's sword from them. This information will succeed in turning Saul's suspicions from his men to the priests (see 1 Sam. 22:9,l0). And Saul, now devoid of all reason, will send for the priests, maliciously interrogate them and have them and everyone connected with them murdered (see 1 Sam. 22:11-19).

In these actions Saul's anger will take on a very primitive form. He will act like a man who cannot confront his wife and so beats the children or the dog. His conduct will be erratic and he will imagine plots against his life.

How to Preserve Emotional Stability

The question remains, What could Saul have done to preserve his emotional stability? Were options open to him that would have prevented the kind of irrational behavior which characterized his life?

In answering these questions it should be pointed out that Saul had indeed experienced some real misfortunes. To be sure, they were of his own making but this does not make them any less real. When he was first told that his dynasty would not continue and then later confronted with the fact that God had rejected him as king over Israel, his response could have been the same as Samuel's. When Samuel faced rejection he sought the Lord in prayer and submitted to His will (see chap. 3). By acknowledging

110

God's sovereignty and yielding himself in obedience to God's overriding providence, Saul's emotional equilibrium could have been preserved.

As with many people today, Saul probably grew to manhood feeling that any show of anger was tantamount to loss of control and that such loss of control would be severely punished.[6] For this reason he was afraid to confront people in an assertive but non-angry way. Instead, he harbored resentment, increased the amount of poison in the reservoir of slush which was building up inside of him, and finally lost touch with reality. All of this was expressed in his warped and perverted sense of judgment.

Accept Anger as a Natural Emotion

As we look for guidance on how to handle anger we find that the apostle Paul has some wise counsel. In Ephesians 4:26 we read, *In your anger do not sin: do not let the sun go down when you are still angry.* In analyzing Paul's statement we find that anger is natural. We all experience it and we should not repress it. By finding appropriate ways of expressing our angry feelings we will avoid the accumulation of slush. By accepting our angry feelings without harsh judgment or moralizing we will be able to handle our emotions without giving the devil an opportunity to obtain control of us. This acceptance of our feelings plus the freedom to express ourselves verbally in a non-destructive way allows us to preserve our emotional stability.

Deal with Anger When We First Experience It

In handling anger, timing is important. By repressing his feelings, Saul "cooled off," but he allowed things to fester inside of him. Only when the abscess had grown to abnormal proportions did it burst. Notice the duration of time he sat under the tree at Michmash, the interval between the Goliath incident and the song of the women, and the period which intervened between Jonathan's counseling his father

111

and Saul's second attempt to kill David. And even after David fled the country there was an interval between his departure and Saul's learning about the action of the priests of Nob. During these intervals much of Saul's anger appeared to lose its abrasive edge. The issues, however, became clouded and distorted. He never realized that the time to deal with his anger was when he first experienced it. And we, by monitoring our emotions, can shorten the time between our first feeling of anger and our later response. Ideally, we can come to a place in our experience where we are so in touch with our emotions that the moment we feel the first signs of anger our mental faculties will respond in an appropriate way.

Accept God's Will Even When It Conflicts with Ours

People invariably become angry over things that have some special meaning for them. In Saul's instance it was his throne and his dynasty. He really cared about himself and his son and, to a lesser extent, his people. It was natural for him to feel the hurt of rejection when God set him aside in favor of someone else. Saul went astray when he did not accept the will of God and was unprepared to live under its mandate. And the same is true of each one of us when we deliberately choose to set God's will aside in favor of our own plans and ambitions.

Forgive and Forget

The old cliche "forgive and forget" is still the best counsel when handling anger. But forgiving involves recognizing and verbalizing our anger, at least to ourselves and to God. We cannot forgive and forget when we harbor a massive slush fund in our hearts. When someone offends us, when we feel frustrated, hurt or rejected, our anger must be experienced, dissipated and ended by forgiving and forgetting what has taken place. This is what the Lord Jesus commanded in the Gospels (see Matt. 5:24; 6:12-15). This

112

is the only true remedy if we expect to enjoy proper mental health. Long-standing grudges become extremely corrosive to our personalities and damage our interpersonal relationships. Ultimately the repression of anger will be accompanied by mild to severe paranoia and destroy all the good that we have sought to do in our lifetimes.

This type of experience is not the product of a moment. It takes years to accumulate and, tragically, is manifest in its most advanced forms in our later years. It blights our old age, leaving us bitter and disillusioned. The only satisfactory way of handling this kind of problem is to put into practice the words of the Lord Jesus. He said, *When you pray, if you hold anything against anyone, forgive him, so that your Father in heaven may forgive you your sins* (Mark 11:25; compare Matt. 6:14,15; Luke 6:37).

Both David and Jonathan were given cause to feel the anger of resentment and frustration. As we shall see, neither of them harbored grudges and their lives are a continuous reminder of how we too may walk in holiness and righteousness in spite of outward pressure and the most uncongenial circumstances.

Interaction

1. From your own experience (as well as from what you have read in this chapter), list some of the ways you have handled frustration, humiliation, and rejection in the past. Were these "healthy" or merely "socially acceptable" methods of repressing your feelings? What would you now do differently?
2. Analyze Saul's attempts to kill David. Why do you think his plans were frustrated? What could he have done?
3. How do you think David felt on his wedding day when Merab was given to someone else? In what ways would you be tempted to act if this happened to you? Do you think Saul expected David to act irresponsibly?
4. By all standards the massacre of the priests of Nob was tragic. How do you explain Saul's irrational action? Is there anyone

113

you know who, on occasions, gives way to fits of uncontrollable temper? What is the best method of dealing with people such as this?

5. God provided us with a model of forgiveness—Himself. He uses different figures to describe *forgiving* and *forgetting* (see Ps. 103:12; Isa. 38:17; Mic. 7:19). The basis of His forgiveness and its extent are described in passages like Hosea 14:4; Ephesians 4:32; Hebrews 10:17. In view of all this, what should be our response to Him? And in the light of His example, how should we relate to others (Matt. 18:22)?

Footnotes

1. "Saul must have been living in fearful expectation of being overthrown by a competitor, an outcome clearly predicted by Samuel. Since the king's own anointment had been a secret one, he could assume that his rival would also be chosen in the same fashion. Saul would therefore have no actual way of knowing who would displace him." This would make him suspicious of anyone whose abilities rivaled his own. See D. Zeligs, *Psychoanalysis and the Bible*, p. 145.

2. The root form of the word means "to cause to bubble up," hence to pour forth words abundantly. *Nabo* is frequently used of prophetic utterances and the *KJV* translators translated the verse with this thought in mind. In view of the context, *"An evil spirit from the LORD came upon Saul . . . ,"* it seems preferable to conclude that the verbal expression was part of the king's mania. (See the LXX where *mainesthai* is used.)

3. Another example of an improper fear-object. See Maurice Wagner's *Put It All Together* (Grand Rapids: Zondervan, 1974), pp. 31,48,49.

4. Merab should have been given to David after he killed Goliath (1 Sam. 17:50,51).

5. How different Saul's situation would have been if he, as with Jonathan, had learned how to handle rejection. As we found earlier, Samuel was set aside by the people because he was "too old" to be their leader. The saintly man continued in his role as prophet and established at Ramah *Naioth*, or dwellings, which made up the "college" and common residence of those who were enrolled in "the school of the prophets." In God's estmate, "rejection" in one sphere of activity does not preclude our serving in another!

6. Zeligs, pp. 138f.

10

MOOD OF THE TIMES

1 SAMUEL 18:1-5; 19:1-10; 20:1-3; 23:16-18

"Friendship," said Aristotle, "is a single soul dwelling in two bodies."[1]

At one time lasting intimate friendships were highly valued, and men such as Ralph Waldo Emerson, Samuel Johnson and William Penn wrote extensively on the subject. Now, in the years since World War II, a change has taken place.

In a brilliant analysis of the changing American character entitled *The Lonely Crowd*, David Riesman writes of this change. He shows that our society is no longer "inner-directed." We no longer have internalized principles to guide us; and now, particularly in our metropolitan areas, the prevailing attitude has become one of "other-directedness." We are more interested in what others think of us than we are in right and wrong. Our concern is how our actions will affect our acceptance by our associates. As a consequence we are shallower in our relationships—self-indulgent, friendly but uncertain of ourselves and our values, and more demanding of approval than people in other countries.[2]

In developing his views, Dr. Riesman points out that our security is no longer derived from spiritual realities. Instead, our reliance is on the government for its support and on membership with different organizations and unions for protection. In place of a former internalized strength of character, Americans are now searching for external standards. These ever-changing standards are determined by our social milieu and this serves to further feed the fires of our insecurity.

In analyzing the situation facing us today, Dr. Riesman links the emergence of this new social character with the decline of Christianity. This decline was in evidence long before World War II. In fact, it was already far advanced by the time of the Fundamentalist-Modernist controversy of the 1920s. The war served only to bring the seeds of incipient spiritual decline to fruition.

But why should we become so concerned with the superficiality of our relationships or an evident change in our system of values? If we're happy and contented with life, what more do we want?

Years ago one of Job's friends spoke of the difficulties we all face. Picturing the open fire which warmed shepherds out on the hills at night, he said, *Man is born to trouble as the sparks fly upward* (Job 5:7). It is in the crises of life that our relationships with others take on new importance (see Prov. 17:17; 18:24). It is then that we need the reassuring hand of a true friend.

In all of recorded history there is no friendship more praiseworthy than the friendship of Jonathan and David. Their relationship illustrates for us the areas in which real friendship may function and how it may strengthen us as we face the ups and downs of life.

116

Basis for Friendship
1 Samuel 18:1-5

Jonathan and David meet for the first time after the young shepherd, still smelling of the sheep, killed Goliath (18:1-5). He is brought before Saul, and *the soul of Jonathan is knit[3] to the soul of David, and Jonathan loves him as himself. . . . And Jonathan makes a covenant with David . . . and Jonathan strips himself of the robe which is on him and gives it to David, with his armor, including his sword and his bow and his belt* (18:1-4).

As we weigh the words of David to Saul before the duel with Goliath (see 1 Sam. 17:31-40; probably spoken in Jonathan's presence, 1 Sam. 20:2), we find that they exhibit a quality of character which would at once endear him to Saul's son. And when Jonathan sees that his actions match his words, the depths of Jonathan's personality respond to the depths of David's own spirit. Their affections are "knit" together by bonds of unalloyed mutual love and esteem,[4] and their friendship expresses itself in a commitment based upon *respect, compatibility* and *shared ideals.*

It is significant that it is Jonathan, the prince and heir apparent to the throne, who takes the initiative. And in expressing his love for David he gives him such gifts[5] as can only be construed as a mark of special honor (compare Gen. 41:39-43; Esther 6:6-9)!

As the months pass their friendship matures. They encourage and strengthen one another as they share life's experiences (compare Heb. 10:24). Jonathan shows no envy as David increases in stature and in popularity with the people (18:5-7,14-16). Their friendship is undergirded by personal, moral and spiritual principles.

Marks of Friendship
1 Samuel 19:1-10; 20:1-3

We have no means of knowing how much time elapsed between chapters 18 and 19. We do know that David

117

served in Saul's army where he became a commander and led Saul's men to victory in several notable engagements. Later, he was appointed Saul's personal bodyguard. However, when Saul became jealous of the young warrior and began to plot his death, David was transferred back to the army where he faced continual danger in combat.

It is when Saul openly begins to plan David's assassination that Jonathan plays the part of an *intercessor* (19:1-7). As soon as he learns of his father's intentions he warns David of the imminent danger facing him. Then, approaching his father, he intercedes on David's behalf. His words are full of tender concern and wise counsel: *Do not let the king sin against his servant David, since he has not sinned against you, and since his deeds have been very beneficial to you. For he took his life in his hands and struck the Philistine, and the LORD brought about a great deliverance for all Israel; and you saw it and rejoiced. Why then should you sin against innocent blood, by putting David to death?* (19:4,5).

Jonathan's tactful handling of this potentially difficult situation shows the extent to which he is guided by strong inner principles. In contrast to people of our day, he was concerned with right and wrong. While it has become fashionable today to conform to the status quo, avoid "making waves," and respond to "signals" from already established power structures within our society, Jonathan shows us that it is patently wrong to be guided by these external standards. By taking a stand for what he believed to be right, and guided by principle rather than expediency, Jonathan was able to secure David's return to court. His father was moved by his sincerity and promised *As the LORD lives, he shall not be put to death* (19:6).

But Jonathan's father is not well. Before long he is seized by one of his fits, and in agitated depression again tries to kill David (19:8-10). David escapes to Samuel, and when Saul pursues him to Ramah, he flees from there to Jonathan

(1 Sam. 20). In the presence of his friend he inquires, *What have I done? What is my iniquity? And what is my sin before your father, that he is seeking my life?* (20:1).

In David's attitude we glimpse another characteristic of true friendship: vulnerability. David lays bare his heart. He exposes his motives and conduct to Jonathan for evaluation. He feels secure in Jonathan's presence and is confident that he can *trust* him with the most intimate details of his life.

In David, Jonathan has his most formidable rival. The throne belongs to him by right of succession. To befriend David is to offend his father and jeopardize his own interests.

If Jonathan had been living today, peer-group pressure would have counseled, "Remain neutral. Steer a middle course. Avoid being drawn into conflicting relationships. Keep your own future in mind. Look out for 'Number One.' "[6] David is bewildered and afraid. His own estimate of the situation is that *there is hardly a step between me and death* (20:3). Jonathan, however, cannot believe that his father has so soon gone back on his promise (19:6). In order to determine the real state of affairs he and David devise a simple plan to test Saul's intentions. Unfortunately, their plan miscarries and Jonathan is placed in *imminent danger* (20:23). He finally realizes that there can be no reconciliation between David and his father.

But if Jonathan was so convinced of right and wrong, why didn't he leave the court and throw in his lot with David? One of the keynotes of a genuine friendship is the willingness to sacrifice all for the sake of the one held in such high esteem. Did Jonathan fail this test of his friendship?

There are some writers who believe that Jonathan made a grave mistake by staying with Saul. One states emphatically, "But for God's king, suffering must precede glory . . . Jonathan fails in the path of discipleship because he does

119

not break with the city and go out with David ... and because he refused to suffer with David he did not reign with him."[7]

We may well ask, What deep spiritual truths were being compromised? Was some important doctrine at stake?

Jonathan knows he will never ascend the throne and that in persecuting David, Saul is further resisting the will of God. But by remaining in court, Jonathan is able to be faithful in his duty to both the king and his country while adhering unalterably in *his loyalty* to David. Such a decision requires real discernment and true spiritual maturity.

If Jonathan was indeed caught between opposing loyalties and yet performed his duty fully without compromising his principles, the question remains, do situations ever arise that necessitate our taking a stand, knowing that this will result in the severing of relationships with those with whom we disagree? The obvious answer is, Yes! But this should not happen simply because we cannot get along with others —whether they be numbered among our own family, our friends, church or business associates. Some far more abiding principle is needed—something which is a direct affront to the Person or work of the Lord Jesus Christ, which robs Him of His glory and will implicate us in compromise or the propagation of false doctrine if we continue in our position or relationship. In such instances it is essential that a parting of the ways occur (see 2 Cor. 6:14-18). Such separations, however, should arise over doctrinal or ethical matters and not as a result of personality clashes. Until these are present, quiet perseverance in well-doing is the best course of action to follow.

Blessings and Benefits of Friendship
1 Samuel 23:16-18

As soon as Jonathan brings word of his father's unrelenting anger to David, the latter realizes that he must flee. The two friends share the sorrow of parting and reaffirm their covenant. David's life from this time onwards is marked by trial and difficulty. And because "it is the nature of mortals to kick a man when he is down,"[8] Saul's servants, the men of Ziph (23:19-24; see also 26:1) and the other unnamed informers (see 22:6; 23:7; 24:1), take delight in telling of David's movements. The result is the continued harassment of one whose loyalty should have earned him the undying respect of the people of Israel.

Jonathan is not motivated as the informers are. He loves David and, at a time when the outlook for David is bleak, he takes his life in his hands and visits the young "outlaw" (23:16-18). He knows that David's faith has been tested to the utmost as a result of the years of hardship. Sensing that David is discouraged, Jonathan encourages him in the Lord. *Do not be afraid,* he says; *the hand of Saul my father shall not find you, and you will be king over Israel, and I shall be next to you.*

The psychology of this kind of interaction has only recently come under systematic inquiry. The principles Jonathan employed are of great value to us as we seek to help those who are discouraged. Jonathan turned David's thoughts away from himself to the One who continuously shows Himself strong on behalf of those who put their trust in Him. He turned David's thoughts God-ward and encouraged him to take refuge with Him who is a very present help in time of trouble. He realized that David was in danger of limiting his world of reality to the forces which were even then threatening his life. Jonathan, therefore, reminded him of God's providential care.

When Jonathan and David part company it is for the last time.[9] From this time onward, the prince's footsteps lead toward the slopes of Mount Gilboa. There he will meet an untimely death at the hands of the Philistines (see 1 Sam. 31:1,2). David, however, will never forget his love and friendship. In one of the most touching eulogies ever uttered, he will sing the praises of his friend (see 2 Sam.

1:17-27). In the course of time he will become king over Judah. He will reign for seven and a half years in Hebron.

Then the northern tribes will crown David king over *all* Israel and he will move his capital to Jerusalem. Remembering the love of Jonathan and the covenant they made with one another, he will ask: *Is there yet anyone left in the house of Saul, that I may show him kindness for Jonathan's sake?* He will be told of Jonathan's son, Mephibosheth, and will give instructions that Mephibosheth is to be brought to the palace and eat at the king's table continuously (see 2 Sam. 9:1-12).

Through these events and circumstances David and Jonathan show the blessings and benefits of true, long-lasting, intimate fellowship.

The Faces of Friendship

It is indeed tragic that in the day in which we are living, men and women have set aside the benefits of long-term friendships for shallow, temporary relationships. In place of internalized principles they depend on externalized and ever-changing social norms. They receive direction from their contemporaries and the mass media and feel that they must respond with appropriate behavior if they are to remain "in" with the group and continue to be accepted by them. As a result many have missed the benefits of a relationship such as Jonathan and David enjoyed.

The Bible emphasizes the role of Jonathan in the *crises* David was called upon to face. It is in the crises of life—the passing of a loved one and the loneliness which follows, the losing of a job, an accident, or some other misfortune—that we, too, need friends. It is through the absence of competition, the presence of mutual esteem, the sharing of experiences, and the real empathy of genuine friends that we are strengthened and helped over the rough places in life. And happy are those men and women whose friends are strong in faith and able to encourage them in the Lord when all that is important to them seems to be collapsing.

Our earthly friendships are also designed to lead us into a greater appreciation of the blessings of God's love for us and the possibility of being, as was Abraham, a *friend of God.* Hugh Black pointed out that "a man must discover that there is an infinite in him, which only the Infinite can match and supply . . . so the human heart has ever craved for a relationship, deeper and more lasting than any possible among men, undisturbed by change, unmenaced by death, unbroken by fear, unclouded by doubt. The limitations and losses of earthly friendship are meant to drive us to the higher friendship. Life is an education in love, but the education is not complete until we learn the love of the Eternal."[10]

God made man with instincts, and aspirations, and heart-hunger, and divine unrest that He might give him full satisfaction in Himself. If we fail to accept His offer of friendship in Christ and do not cultivate this relationship, then we miss the very best life affords. Only His friendship can fully meet our deepest needs. The weary, the lonely, the starved heart of man, oppressed as many are with burdens and longings, cares and anxieties, can only find rest and peace through intimate fellowship with Jesus Christ (see Matt. 11:27-29).[11]

And all that Jonathan meant to David, the Lord Jesus can mean to us. By walking with Him we are enriched and blessed, our spirits are elevated and purified and our innermost being is transformed and beautified. He it is who said, *No longer do I call you servants; for a servant does not know what his Master is doing; but I have called you friends* (John 15:15). *You are my friends if you do what I command you* (John 15:14). And, *this is my commandment that you love one another* (John 15:12). (See also John 13:34,35; 14:15, 21-23.) In this ennobling friendship "we part from men to meet with God, that we may be able to meet men again on a higher platform."[12]

123

Interaction

1. From what you know of the background of Jonathan and David, what did they share in common? How did this influence their system of values? Why did Jonathan invariably take the lead in their relationship?

2. David was Jonathan's most formidable rival. What kept Jonathan from jealousy or from taking advantage of David's misfortunes?

3. In what ways is mass media projecting an image that shallow, impermanent relationships are the "in" thing? Which TV series have you watched recently that portrays either a single man or a single woman going from one temporary relationship to another each week? What effect is this having (a) on you and your family relationships, and (b) on your children and their future attitudes toward love and marriage?

4. What do you think of this statement by Dr. Riesman in *The Lonely Crowd:* "Since the other-directed types [of people] are to be found among the young, in the larger cities, and among the upper income groups, we may assume that, *unless present trends are reversed,* the hegemony [dominance] of other-direction lies not far off"? (p. 21, italics added) Is this an evidence of spiritual decline? How will this affect our relationships with other believers?

5. Consider the privilege and responsibility of friendship in John 15:13-17. What difference will this kind of relationship make in your life-style?

Footnotes

1. Diogenes Laertius, *Aristotle,* V:20.
2. D. Riesman, *The Lonely Crowd* (New Haven: Yale University Press, 1950).
3. The Hebrew *kasar,* "to bind," in the Niphal means "to join, to knot." It is used in 1 Samuel 18:1 to describe the bond of love between Jonathan and David (see Gen. 44:30 where the same word is used).
4. The extremely foolish notion that the love of Jonathan and David (see

1 Sam. 18:1; 2 Sam. 1:26) stemmed from a homosexual relationship is too ludicrous to require refutation. Homosexuality (referred to as sodomy) is condemned in the Scriptures (Lev. 18:22; 20:13; Deut. 23:17; Rom. 1:27; 1 Cor. 6:9; etc.). See W.G. Cole's *Sex and Love in the Bible* (New York: Association, 1959), and R. Patai's *Sex and Family in the Bible and the Middle East* (Garden City: Doubleday, 1959).

5. This is what Saul should have done. After David defeated Goliath, Saul should have lavished on him gifts commensurate with his victory. All of this he failed to do.

6. See Riesman, pp. 22,26.

7. John Watt, *Old Testament Characters* (New York: Loizeaux, n.d.), pp. 112,113.

8. Aeschylus, *Agamemnon*, I:884.

9. W.G. Blaikie, *The First Book of Samuel*, pp. 326,327.

10. Hugh Black, *Friendship* (New York: Revell, 1903), p. 223.

11. See B.B. Warfield, *The Person and Work of Christ* (Philadelphia: Presbyterian and Reformed, 1950), pp. 104-106.

12. Black, p. 227.

11

SHAKING THE FOUNDATIONS

1 SAMUEL 17:25-28; 18:17-30; 19:1-17; 20:1—22:23

A recent newspaper article carried a tragic story of child abuse. It dwelt at length on the bruises and burn marks found on the child's body and alluded to the tragic mental and emotional state in which this seven-year-old girl was found. This story brought to mind another incident—this time, of a youth who had suffered unbelievably harsh discipline under tyrannical parents. Now, 25 years later, he is married and trying to correct the impression of these injustices as he attempts to rear his own children with love and discretion.

Within recent weeks a young wife and mother contacted a Christian counselor. From the beginning he realized that her distress was very real. "My husband is away from home a great deal," she confided; ". . . sometimes for several weeks at a time. The children and I see very little of him. We look forward to his return, but when he comes home he acts as if we aren't there." During the conversation she told the counselor that at first she blamed herself for his disinterest. More recently, however, she learned that another woman had entered his life. She felt very keenly the wrong done both to her and her children.

During the time of discussion following a Bible study in a suburban home, one member felt led to share his problem with those who were present. He was frustrated. He worked hard at his job and resented the fact that his boss frequently picked on him in front of his colleagues. Even when an error had nothing to do with the work he was doing, he got the blame.

One after another, the members of the group offered suggestions with most of them advocating that he resign. (The high unemployment rate in his area made this an unwise move.) But none of the members of the group made any suggestions of how he might handle the injustices which were such an integral part of his life.

While injustice wears many masks, the strength of its attack lies in our vulnerability. It may be directed either against our identity—our sense of belonging, worth, or ability—or the limitation of our personal freedom. Examples of injustice—social, economic or domestic—are not hard to find. We have all experienced them at one time or another. The problem we all face is that if we do not handle our emotional responses properly, we will become bitter and resentful. Ultimately we will find that these unresolved feelings have ground cinders into our souls.

How then are we to handle unfair treatment, discriminatory conduct, or infringements on our liberty? Is our experience the same as Claudian's when he wrote, "When I observe [in] the affairs of men . . . the guilty flourishing in continuous happiness, and the righteous tormented, my religion, tottering, begins once more to fall"?[1] Does the Christian have no answer to the inequities of life?

Once again David illustrates the mountain peaks and dark valleys of our experience (see Rom. 15:4), so that we might learn how to handle our emotional responses to the injustices we face.

The Injustice of Broken Promises
1 Samuel 17:25-28; 18:17-19

The first injustice David is called upon to face concerns Saul's broken promise. When David killed Goliath, he and the men in Saul's army knew that the victor was to be given great riches, be granted the king's daughter as his wife, and be made free from taxation (17:25-28). But with the external threat removed, Saul quickly forgot his pledge.

Such treatment is not without its parallel today. A man with whom we worked for many years performed great service to his employers. In a time of crisis he assumed *pro tem* a vacant vice president's position and, by means of his unique ability, brought the company from the brink of bankruptcy to fiscal responsibility. The crisis over, however, the board turned its back on the unique contribution he had made to the organization and selected someone else as their vice president. Such thankless indifference caused the young administrator to feel that he had been used. He became bitter and ultimately left the company.

In David's case further injustices are heaped upon him. These are traceable to his growing popularity with the people and Saul's increasing jealousy. Saul looks upon David as a threat to his tottering security and determines to do away with him. His plan is diabolical. He offers David the hand of his daughter, Merab, in marriage, on the condition that he will continue to distinguish himself in battle (18:17). This David does, but without any of the reckless daring which another young man might resort to in order to impress a prospective father-in-law or the girl of his choice (see 18:30). He neither shows resentment for having been denied Merab after killing Goliath nor does he exhibit the insecurity which would tempt him to impress others with his ability. He has a strong personal identity. He is

128

confident in the Lord and confident in himself.

Unfortunately for David, when the wedding day dawns, Merab (though legally betrothed to David and, by Jewish law, regarded as his wife[2]) is given to someone else (18:19).

The natural reaction of a young man to such a breach of faith (not to mention the *insult* such rejection implied) would be to display his resentment in some reckless manner. And certainly this is what Saul expected. David, however, behaves himself wisely. His conduct is in contrast to that of one young man, who, when jilted by his fiancee went out and got drunk. No such indiscretion marks David's conduct. His inner orientation and implicit faith in God's all-wise providence keeps him from falling into Saul's trap. His eyes are on the Lord (see Ps. 16:8), and this internal motivation preserves him from unwise actions. Had he been eager for position, honor or prestige (see 18:18), or motivated by fleshly concerns, the story might very well have had a different ending.

The Injustice of Evil for Good
1 Samuel 18:20-29; 19:1-17

Realizing that his first plan has failed, Saul tries another. He learns of his younger daughter's interest in David (18:20) and instructs his servants to approach David with a proposition (18:22-26). The mention of *today* in verse 21 and *the days were not expired* in verse 26 indicates that Saul set a short, specific time limit in which the feat of bravery was to be performed. He hoped that David would be killed as he tried to carry out a dangerous assignment.

David more than satisfies Saul's wish for a "dowry"[3] and, realizing that he cannot sidestep the issue this time, Saul gives Michal to David in marriage (18:27-29).

In David, Saul's anger finds a scapegoat. The greater David's success in battle, the greater becomes the king's fear of the youth whom he now regards as his competitor for the throne (see 1 Sam. 13:14; 15:17-23). His anger, therefore, finds an outlet in plotting David's assassination (1 Sam. 19:1-17). On one occasion Jonathan intervenes, but the truce is only temporary. Saul does not realize that in his unbalanced frame of mind he is rewarding David's faithful service with evil instead of good.

When war breaks out again David achieves another military victory. Immediately upon his return to court *an evil spirit* troubles Saul. David tries to soothe the king's distraught feelings, but Saul, seizing the opportunity to be rid of his rival, throws his spear at David. The spear misses its intended mark and strikes the wall with such force that it becomes embedded in it (19:8-10).

David's response to such injustice is *not* to return anger for anger (see 1 Pet. 3:9). His military prowess is such that he could easily have staged a *coup.* And knowing that he is destined by God to be the king, he could have rationalized removing Saul's head from his shoulders with the same ease as he had Goliath's. Instead of retaliation (see Ps. 94:1; Rom. 12:19), and out of respect for Saul as the anointed of the Lord, David refrains from any self-vindicating acts. He realizes that his times are in God's hands (see Ps. 31:15). His internal-orientation preserves his mental and emotional balance. He leaves Saul's presence and after going to Michal (19:11-17), escapes to Samuel.

Psalm 59 is attributed to this period of David's life. It gives us a picturesque description of those whom Saul sent to watch David's home. It also describes in clear and unmistakable terms this young man's reliance upon God during these trying times. Instead of the despair which anxiety frequently produces, there is recognition of the sin done to him and an expression of the quiet confidence that God will continue to be his *high tower [his defense, and his] refuge in the day of his distress* (59:16).

In facing these injustices David shows us that his sense of *worth* has not been impaired by the events which have taken place. When Saul insulted him by giving Merab to

130

Adriel he felt no need to assert himself in order to reestablish his feeling of strength and independence. He had long since submitted to the Lord and drew his strength from Him. And when Saul tried on more than one occasion to kill him, it would have been easy for him to feel *rejected*. To be sure Saul improperly rewarded him for his labors, but David's recognition of his standing before God kept him from becoming materialistically minded. He realized that his true recompense would come from the God whom he served. As a result, he continued to behave himself wisely; and when he was compelled to leave his young bride and flee for his life, he relied on the Lord for comfort and security.

David shows us that inner principles (rather than outward symbols such as wealth, honor, prestige) and absolute reliance upon the sovereignty of God are the only sure way to combat the injustices we all face at one time or another.

The Injustice of Persecution
1 Samuel 19:18-24; 20:1—22:23

After leaving Michal, David flees to Samuel (19:18-24; see Pss. 6; 7; 11).[4] Perhaps in the relative security of this retreat he relaxes his spiritual defenses. When soldiers begin to arrive and then Saul himself appears, David becomes afraid. His proper fear-object (the Lord) is replaced by an improper fear-object.

God, however, is caring for David. Saul comes under such constraint of the Spirit that he strips off his outer clothing[5] and lies on his face before the Lord until morning (19:24). This gives David time to make his escape.

But where shall he go? To whom can he turn for help?

In desperation David turns to Jonathan. He opens his heart to him and when Jonathan protests his father's innocence David suggests a way to test the king's true feelings (20:4-7). His plan, however, involves Jonathan in a deliberate lie. It also places Jonathan in grave danger. The result of this practiced falsehood has been described by Dr. J.C. Geikie: "Every hope [of reconciliation with Saul] is speedily dashed. Jonathan's apology for David kindles [Saul's] fury. Accusing his son of treachery . . . he demands that David be sent for . . . [Jonathan's] respectful remonstrance only shows the depths of the king's hatred, for it is answered by hurling his javelin at the speaker."[6]

Jonathan narrowly escapes death and leaves the king's presence in anger. The next morning he meets with David and confirms his friend's suspicions. David, the loyal soldier and son-in-law of Saul, cannot even return home to see his wife. He must escape or else be discovered by one of Saul's servants.

David's trials are only beginning. He feels the pangs of anxiety and loneliness. With the Sabbath[7] approaching, and fearing lest he be seen, he makes his way to Ahimelech the high priest (21:1-9; see Ps. 52). On arriving at Nob, Ahimelech's greeting is guarded, and David tells another situational lie: *The king has commissioned me with a matter*, he says, *and he has said to me, Let no one know anything about the matter on which I am sending you and with which I have commissioned you; and I have directed the young men to a certain place. Now, therefore, what [food] do you have on hand?* (21:2,3).

Ahimelech gives David the Bread of the Presence,[8] which has only recently been taken from the tabernacle, and also Goliath's sword (21:6,8,9). And leaving Nob, David flees from the land of Benjamin to the borders of Philistia.[9] Unfortunately, he is seen by Doeg (v. 7) and when Doeg reports to Saul all that Ahimelech did for David, Ahimelech and the entire priestly village are massacred (22:6-23).[10]

It is probable that David uses the Sabbath to make good his escape.[11] He is still dominated by fear and wearied with Saul's relentless persecution. But going to Gath, a city outside the land given to his forefathers, can only be construed as a lapse of faith. The spiritual heritage of the Hebrews was so intimately connected with the land[12] that to leave it without divine warrant was regarded as showing lack of confidence in the Lord.

David's reception by Achish, king of Gath, must have been cordial enough, but when the king's servants recount David's exploits Achish's attitude toward David changes (21:10,11). Once again the young outlaw fears for his life (see Ps. 56). He is, to all intents and purposes, imprisoned in the city. He therefore pretends to be insane and when his saliva runs down his beard[13] he is judged *non compos mentis* by the Philistines (21:12-15; see Ps. 34). Only then is he sent away (22:1). In one of his Psalms, David describes this as an *escape* and gladly makes his way to the cave of Adullam (see Pss. 57; 142). There men gather about him until his band numbers about 400. Among those who resort to David is Gad, the prophet (22:4,5). Next to Samuel he seems to have stood highest in David's esteem and David must have regarded him as a special gift from the Lord— one by means of whom he could learn the divine will and with whom he could have intimate fellowship now that he could no longer have free interaction with Jonathan.

Our Response to Injustice

But what is there in these events for us?

It has been said that trials never weaken us, they only show us that we are weak. Through his experiences David came to know his own weaknesses and learned firsthand the danger of taking his eyes off the Lord. Left to himself he resorted to carnal expediency. The events through which he passed showed him the wretchedness of such self-dependence. And following his experience at Gath, he came to trust once more in the protection of God. Then with renewed confidence he could sing, *O taste and see that the LORD is good; happy is the man who takes refuge in Him* (Ps. 34:8).

Through David's experience we learn something of what it is to suffer wrongfully, to be unjustly deprived of love and companionship of one's wife and trusted friend, and to be forced to endure social ostracism and economic hardship. Under such conditions of anxiety, loneliness, and the constant fear of betrayal, the strongest heart would fail and the most stoic spirit would be inclined to give way to either resentment or despair.

David shows us that the response to injustice is never to seek revenge nor to doubt God's providence. Our response to injustice must come from our own identity—the way we feel about ourselves. First, it must be rooted in a strong *sense of belonging* to God the Father, so that no matter what storms arise we trust ourselves entirely to His care. The greater our appreciation of His sovereignty the more likely we will be to accept His will for our lives, and the easier we will be able to keep our problems in perspective.

Second, our response to injustice must also be supported by a very real *sense* of our *worth as individuals.* To believers, this comes directly from our relationship with the Lord Jesus Christ (see 1 Pet. 1:18). The more we come to understand the privilege and benefits of Christ's love for us and our value to Him, the more clearly will earthly things be seen in their proper light. This will enable us, from the firm foundation of our union with Christ (see Col. 3:3; Heb. 13:5-7), to face loss and rejection, insults and misunderstanding.

Finally, we can model ourselves after the heroes of faith (see Heb. 11), because the Holy Spirit works in us to accomplish His purpose. Through His inner working we are given the *ability or feeling of competence*—to face each God-appointed task with confidence, no matter how difficult it may appear. While we may on occasion succumb to external pressure as David did, this should not and need not be the norm, for we are not expected to live in defeat. Instead, by means of the Holy Spirit's indwelling, we may lay hold of His almighty power (see Jas. 4:6-8,10; 1 John 4:4).

With such resources we need not pretend to be something we are not or become so consumed with earthly temporalities that we forget eternal realities. David was not locked into a materialistic view of life, neither was he hedonistic. The psalms he wrote during this period of his life give evidence of his belief in God's program for him and the fact that God's plan would be worked out in his experience regardless of his outward circumstances (see Rom. 8:28,31-37). The hardships he endured were serving to bring him to greater maturity (see Eph. 4:13). This, too, was the apostle Paul's experience as he faced the injustices of those who opposed his ministry (see 2 Cor. 1:8); and it can be ours as well as we face the inequities of life (see 1 Pet. 1:7; 2 Cor. 3:18—4:2,17,18). With Paul we may say with confidence, *But thanks be to God, who always leads us in triumph in Christ* (2 Cor. 2:14).

Interaction

1. What unfair practices have you felt most keenly? Were they social, economic, or family-related? How did you react to them? Was your reaction motivated by personal considerations?

2. The injustices Saul heaped on David were compounded when David was forced to leave his wife and home, and flee for his life. How did he grapple with anxiety, fear and loneliness? What turned his sorrow to praise (Ps. 34:8)?

3. In what subtle ways does our desire for position, honor or possessions add weight to the injustices others may do to us?

4. Why did David fail after visiting Samuel at Ramah? What may we learn from his experience?

5. In Colossians 2:9,10 the apostle Paul says that *in Christ dwells all the fullness of the Godhead bodily, and you have been brought into that fullness [by virtue of your union with Him].* What practical application does this truth have to (a) your

135

sense of belonging, or security; to (b) your worth as an individual; and (c) your ability or feeling of competence?

Footnotes

1. Claudin, *In Rufinum*, I, 1, 12.

2. Merrill F. Unger, "Marriage," *Unger's Bible Dictionary*, p. 698; Roland de Vaux, *Ancient Israel*, pp. 32,33.

3. See de Vaux's discussion of the *mohar*, "dowry," in *Ancient Israel*, p. 28.

4. J. Cunningham Geikie, *Hours with the Bible* (London: Hodder and Stoughton, 1882), III, 152 ff.; Alexander McLaren, *The Life of David Reflected in His Psalms* (Grand Rapids: Baker, 1955), pp. 70-85.

5. W.G. Blaikie, *The First Book of Samuel*, pp. 314-316. Many versions translated the Hebrew *arom* as "naked." Such, however, is not the case. Only the discarding of the outer garments is in view. The usage of the word does not apply to the long linen tunic worn next to the skin.

6. Geikie, III, 149.

7. The Sabbath would begin at 6:00 P.M. on Friday evening.

8. See "Showbread," in *Unger's Bible Dictionary*, p. 1066.

9. Nob was about one mile from Saul's capital at Gibeah and Gath is fairly close at hand, but in Philistia and out of Saul's domain. See *Macmillan Bible Atlas*, p. 90.

10. The comments of John Davis, *The Birth of a Kingdom* (Grand Rapids: Baker, 1970), pp. 80-82; and John Kitto, *Daily Bible Illustrations* (Edinburgh: W. Oliphant, 1873), III, 256-259, on David's "situational lie" and Saul's diabolical act are worth noting.

11. The emphasis on *"that day"* in I Samuel 21:10 supports this view. The principle underlying Ahimelech's giving David the Showbread and David's travels on the Sabbath is that when a *ceremonial* obligation comes into collision with a *moral* duty or necessity, the lesser obligation is to give place to the greater. See W.G. Blaikie, *The First Book of Samuel*, p. 334.

12. See W.H. Griffith Thomas, *Genesis* (Grand Rapids: Eerdmans, 1966), pp. 118ff.

13. A man's beard was regarded with reverence. Men sometimes swore by their beards. To defile one's beard (as David did by allowing saliva to run down onto it) was regarded as a sure sign of madness.

12

THE REFINER'S FIRE

1 SAMUEL 23:1—24:22; 26:1-25

Shakespeare may have had the words of James (1:2-8),
our Lord's brother, in mind when he wrote:
Sweet are the uses of adversity;
Which, like a toad, ugly and venomous,
Wears yet a precious jewel in its head;
And this your life, exempt from public haunt,
Finds tongues in trees, books in running brooks,
Sermons in stones, and good in everything.[1]
Yet most of us treat trials as unwelcome guests. Because we
must all face the many and varied problems of life we
should take courage from the apostle Paul. He wrote the
Christians in Rome and said:
*Through him [Christ] we have confidently entered into
this new relationship of grace . . . . We can be full of joy here
and now even in our trials and troubles. Taken in the right
spirit these very things will give us patient endurance; this
in turn will develop a mature character, and a character of
this sort produces a steady hope, a hope that will never*

disappoint us (Rom. 5:4,5, *Phillips;* see Col. 1:10,11). Peter exhorted his readers not to give way to despair when faced with various difficulties. *For this very reason*, he said, *you must do your utmost from your side, and see that your faith carries with it real goodness of life. Your goodness must be accompanied by knowledge, your knowledge by self-control, your self-control by the ability to endure. Your endurance too must always be accompanied by devotion to [a real trust in] God* (2 Pet. 1:5-7, *Phillips*). The problems that beset us are designed to help us grow spiritually. The difficulties we face insure that we neither become complacent nor unproductive. By responding positively to hardships we develop steadfastness of purpose and the grace of God can be seen in our lives.

David was prepared for service as Israel's king by working through the adversity he encountered. As with the Lord Jesus, he came to full maturity[2] as a result of the things he suffered (see Heb. 2:10).

Tried by Ingratitude
1 Samuel 23:1-12

Having suffered severely at the hand of Saul, David now hopes to be left in peace. After taking his parents to the king of Moab for protection (22:3,4), he and his men settle down outside the borders of Israel. God, however, rebukes him for doing this and, heeding the word of the Lord through the prophet, David and his men return to Judah. They make their camp in the forest of Hereth,[3] nine miles northwest of Hebron (22:5).

It appears as if God brought David back to Judah so that he would learn of a predatory raid of the Philistines on Keilah. He knew that David would respond to the crisis and, by taking up arms on behalf of his people, would prepare himself for greater responsibilities in the future.

When word is brought to David of the Philistine attack on the people of Keilah (23:1), he inquires of the Lord,

138

Shall I go and attack the Philistines? And the Lord answered Go, and attack the Philistines, and deliver Keilah (23:2). David's men, however, are reluctant to expose themselves to fresh danger. Disavowing any obligation to go to the defense of their western neighbors, they complain of the risk (23:3).

David again seeks divine counsel and is told, *Arise, go down to Keilah, for I will deliver the Philistines into your hand* (23:4). He then challenges his men with the task to be done, and in obeying the command of the Lord, they find that their efforts are crowned with success (23:5). The inhabitants of Keilah are jubilant and receive David and his men into the city with great rejoicing. Deliverance from the Philistines saved these agrarian people from almost total economic collapse. To David, the acclaim he and his men receive must have been reminiscent of earlier times (see 1 Sam. 18:7).

It is during David's stay at Keilah that Abiathar the priest, the son of Ahimelech, joins David and his men (23:6; see 22:6-23). He relates to David the destruction of Nob,[4] and David, after openly acknowledging his guilt, takes Abiathar into his service. God has now provided the future king with both a prophet and a priest. It would appear as if David has everything he could wish for: a city in which to live, the gratitude of the people, the appreciative esteem of his men, and two servants of the Lord to minister to him.

But news of David's deliverance of Keilah soon reaches Saul. The deranged monarch seizes the opportunity to trap David inside the city (23:7,8).

As soon as David learns of Saul's intentions he summons Abiathar. He then petitions the Lord regarding the actions of the men of Keilah (23:5-12) and learns that they will most assuredly betray him into Saul's hands. David's attitude is characterized by meekness (23:10-12). Realizing that he serves the God of the covenant and that his God

139

is faithful in all that He does, he readily submits to his Sovereign's will.

The ingratitude of the men of Keliah may have caused a person of lesser caliber to become embittered and disillusioned. David, however, rises above all natural human resentment and without any display of anger quietly leaves the city.

Ingratitude is particularly hard to bear and yet we find it prevailing on every hand. A few years ago the daily papers carried the story of a wealthy bachelor in New York City. He was in the habit of giving literally hundreds of thousands of dollars each year to support promising students in colleges and universities across the land. Having no family, he was particularly lonely at Christmastime. A chance remark was overheard and it led to the article in the paper. This wealthy millionaire said, "After all the money I have given to educate young people, not one of them has remembered me and sent me a Christmas card."

It would have been very easy for this benefactor to become bitter and turn against those who took for granted his beneficence. Fortunately for them he did not. As with David he took their thankless indifference in his stride. He did not allow it to upset his emotional equilibrium.

Strengthened by God
1 Samuel 23:13-18

In the experience of David and his men, they find that they must flee for their lives once more. It is no longer safe for them to return to Adullam or the valley of Elad, or the thickets of Hereth. Saul knows of these retreats. In seeking a suitable refuge they turn south and escape to the neighborhood of Ziph, about four miles southeast of Hebron.

The territory of Ziph is in the hill country of Judah (see Josh. 15:55), nearly 2900 feet above sea level and filled with limestone caves. This area also affords a commanding view of the surrounding country. Two roads pass beneath

the hill, the one leading south to Carmel, Maon and Beer-
sheba, and the other northwest to the central mountain
range of Palestine. In this ideal location David and his men
imagine themselves secure. The people of the southern re-
gion, however, deal treacherously with David and betray
his whereabouts to Saul. The result is that Saul seeks David
daily (23:14). On one occasion he almost has David within
his grasp. David and his men are in Maon, south of Ziph,
in the Arabah.[5] As the noose begins to tighten around them
(23:26), Saul receives an urgent message: *Hurry and come,*
for the Philistines have made a raid on the land (23:27).
And Saul is forced to temporarily abandon his pursuit of
David. This gives his young son-in-law time to escape (see
Ps. 54).

As we ponder the experiences through which David
passed during these months, we might well ask, What kept
deep scars from forming on his soul? A lesser man would
have become cynical and if revenge had been denied him
he would ultimately have had to content himself with justi-
fying his actions while becoming all the time more disillusioned and bitter with life.

David, however, did not become caustic; and while vengeance on the Ziphites would have been easy, as far as we
know, the thought never entered his mind. How then was
he able to preserve his spiritual equilibrium?

David's psalms provide the answer (see Ps. 63). He took
his problems to the Lord. He unburdened himself before
the One who could lift his troubles from him. He candidly
told God all that was on his heart (see Pss. 43: 55). He
neither excused his feelings nor glossed over the wrongs
done him by others. In telling God all that was concerning
him he was preserved from harboring resentment and from
allowing ill-will toward others to fester in his soul. God
became his *fortress,* his *strength,* his *deliverer,* his *shield,*
and the *horn of his salvation* (see Pss. 18: 62).

This attitude of trust and devotion is in keeping with the

advice of the Lord Jesus in Matthew 6:25-34. He told His disciples not to be overly anxious about things in this life. And the apostle Paul, too, gave similar counsel to the Philippians (Phil. 4:6,7). Likewise, Peter, in writing to the believers of his day, encouraged them to cast all their care upon the Lord (1 Pet. 5:7).

And David, with his prayer-life intact and his confidence in the Lord undergirding his heart and mind, is able to make his way from Maon to Engedi, "the Spring of the Goats," on the western edge of the Dead Sea. There beside an oasis, surrounded by desolate wastes and with precipices on three sides, he and his men hope they can elude Saul. David is to learn, however, that the only real security lies in trusting the Lord day by day.

Tempted by Opportunity
1 Samuel 23:19—24:22; 26:1-25

After repulsing the Philistines, Saul follows David to Engedi. His forces outnumber David's 5-to-1. He comes upon David's camp where the sheepfolds are and finding no one there goes into a cave to relieve[6] himself. He is unaware of the fact that David and his men are also in the cave (1 Sam. 24:3). In fact, Saul is so close to David that David can cut off the edge of his robe.

David's men look upon Saul's defenseless position as a God-given opportunity to be rid of their implacable enemy (24:4).[7] David's response to the suggestion that they kill Saul is magnanimous. His words reveal his internal motivation. He acts with complete disregard for his personal safety and, solely on the basis of what is right, restrains his men from taking Saul's life (24:6,7).

David's attitude is in complete contrast to the spirit of the world of today. All too often our young people in school seize upon any and every opportunity to pay back those whom they feel have wronged them. Generally, this is done with interest and the injustice is thereby compounded. And even adults when they feel that they have been wronged will, if given the opportunity, retaliate and attempt to hurt (or even destroy the character of) the one who has offended them. But vengeance must be related to justice, not to some arbitrary whim we may devise. By looking beyond the temporal and bearing in mind spiritual principles, David is able to rise above the temptation to kill Saul.

After Saul arises and leaves the cave, David follows him and, calling after him, shows him the border of his robe. His attitude in addressing Saul is respectful and his words to Saul are direct (24:8-15). He appeals to the great Judge of all and shows that by sparing Saul's life he is guiltless of the charges informers have laid against him.

In all of this David's awareness of reality is remarkable. He knows himself and can therefore act with forbearance towards Saul. He is without ulterior motives and, therefore, can resist the overtures of those who so recently recommended that he kill Saul. And with control of himself he can boldly say to Saul, *I will not stretch out my hand against my lord, for he is the LORD'S anointed* (24:10).

David also knows Saul. He is not naive. He knows that the king is prone to listen to those who are only too willing to slander his son-in-law to him. Listening to them has placed him at enmity with God and God's plan for His people (see 1 Sam. 28:16). In contrast, Saul's response to David's words is in keeping with his character (24:16-22). He is genuinely contrite and acknowledges the high-minded probity of his son-in-law. He also expresses his belief that David will one day be king and entreats him not to exterminate his descendants. David readily agrees to this and Saul returns to his home in Gibeah.

David knows, however, that Saul's remorse will be short-lived. His father-in-law responds to external stimuli and resolutions make no lasting impression on him.

Just as David may have expected, it isn't long before the Ziphites again stir up the king (1 Sam. 26:1). Their calumny arouses Saul's suspicions and inflames his anger. Summoning his army, he departs for Ziph and camps on a hill overlooking Jeshimon.[8]

David sees Saul coming and notes the place where he pitches his camp. At night, when all the soldiers are asleep, David and Abishai steal into Saul's camp. They step carefully over the prostrate forms until they come to Saul. There, standing over Saul's body, Abishai whispers, *Today God has delivered your enemy into your hand; now, therefore, please let me strike him with a spear—even into the ground with one stroke—and I will not need to do it a second time* (26:8; see 1 Chron. 11:20).

Abishai's mention of *today* carries with it the note of urgency, and recalls the fact that Saul had been in David's grasp once before. At Engedi David graciously spared his life. He may have felt that by proving his loyalty, the king would leave him in peace. This Saul promised to do, but the 3000 men about him now give ample proof of his change of heart.

Abishai's next statement, namely, that *God (Elohim) has delivered Saul into your hand*, is also true. But does that mean that David should kill Saul? Other principles enter into the decision-making process. David lives under the covenant and as a result he will not lift up his hand against the LORD'S *(Yahweh's)* anointed. Realizing this, and sensing that David's religious scruples are delaying action, Abishai says, in effect: "Well, if you're not going to kill him, let me do it." But David dissuades him. He knows that the guilt will be equally his, even though the act has been done by someone else.

David then tells Abishai of his confidence. *As the LORD [the God who keeps covenant] lives, surely the LORD will strike him [as He did Nabal], or his day will come that he dies, or he will go down into battle and perish. The LORD forbid that I should stretch out my hand against His anointed* (26:10,11).

Then, taking Saul's spear and water jug, they cross the ravine to the mountain opposite Saul. From this vantage point David calls first to Abner, captain of Saul's body-guard (26:14-16); then he speaks to Saul. His attitude this time is different. He is still courteous and does not indulge in any invective of the king. He does bring to the fore the real issue, even claiming that those who have aroused Saul's jealousy are *cursed before the LORD, for they now have driven him out [of the land] that he should have no attachment with the inheritance of the LORD* (26:19). The territory of Israel is now too small for David. The merciless opposition of those who slandered him has exposed all of his hiding places; there is now nowhere for him to go.

Saul's response to the evidence of David's integrity is the same as before. He acknowledges that he has been a pawn in the hands of others (26:21). His expression of sorrow is sincere but because it is not supported by strong internal convictions it will soon fade. Saul again entreats David's favor, and on this note they part, never to see each other again.

David's Patience—God's Providence

It is well for us to observe that in all of David's dealings with Saul he is motivated by principles which run contrary to the natural instinct of man. Most people in situations similar to David's would naturally seek some form of retaliation. They would attempt to vindicate themselves and, if God's justice appeared to be slow in coming, might even take the law into their own hands.

Two matters in this passage are of particular significance to us. They concern (1) David's patience and (2) God's providence.

David had been promised the kingdom. In many ways David could have justified taking Saul's life and seizing the throne. That he did not act impetuously or indiscreetly is due to his absolute trust in the Lord. He exercised self-restraint even when faced with the utmost provocation. And he was even able to restrain his men when providence seemed to be playing into his hands.

In this respect we have a great deal to learn from David. It is hard for us to wait for God's appointed time. We want everything now. And so we engage in compromises and short-cuts, make rash purchases, rush into marriage, make unwise investments, neglect the real things of life for the trivial, and spend the maturer years of our lives regretting our impatience and indiscretion.

Patience is one of the first lessons we learn in God's school. To prevent discouragement—which often accompanies delay—from having a negative effect on us, we need to have confidence in God's all-wise providence (see 1 Thess. 1:3; Rom. 8:29). In this respect the life of David is a singularly fitting commentary on passages of Scripture such as Proverbs 3:5,6 and Romans 8:28. God was watching over David. When Saul spoke to his servants and to Jonathan and suggested that they kill David, Jonathan was on hand to defend his friend (see 1 Sam. 19:1-6). Later, when Saul hurled a javelin at David, his own nimbleness saved his life. When Saul again tried to kill him, Michal helped him escape and then delayed his pursuers. And when Saul tried to apprehend him at Ramah, the Spirit of God came upon Saul, giving David time to flee to Jonathan. At Keilah he was supernaturally warned of the treachery intended by the men of the city and escaped before Saul could trap him. And at Maon, when David was almost within Saul's grasp, the king was forced to give up pursuit because the Philistines invaded the land.

David's psalms reveal his awareness of God's involvement in the day-to-day affairs of his life. While it was left for great David's greater Son, the Lord Jesus Christ, to give expression to the words, *Thy will be done* (Matt. 6:10), David practiced what He taught in all the harrowing circumstances he faced.

In the statement, *Thy will be done*, we have the element of submission which is so necessary for our mental health and the enjoyment of life. It involves the acknowledgment of God's sovereignty. We trust ourselves entirely to His love with the assurance that He will work all things for our good. While this does not mean that we place the same trust in others as we do in the Lord, it does mean that we refrain from interfering with His plans by taking into our own hands the shaping of our destinies. As with David we are then free to look upon our trials and difficulties as the proving ground by which we are being prepared for our tomorrows. It is, therefore, choice not chance that determines our destiny.

Interaction

1. In what specific ways does the manner in which we handle the day-to-day discouragements of life determine what we will become? How may the teaching of passages such as Romans 5:4,5 be of help to us?

2. Why is our maturity (mental, emotional, spiritual) important (a) to us, and (b) to God? How is it achieved (see Col. 1:10,11; 2 Pet. 1:5-7)?

3. From David's example, what would you conclude would be the best way to handle ingratitude? What value does this have?

4. When others malign us or falsely accuse us our natural reaction is one of retaliation. From what we learn from the psalms how did David handle this kind of abuse?

5. The vicissitudes through which David passed illustrate the sovereign protection of God. Of what value is this to us?

Footnotes

1. William Shakespeare. "As You Like It," Act II, Sc. 1.

2. The Greek *teleios*, translated in the *King James Version* by the word "perfect." means "having attained the end, purpose, or goal." Depending on

the context it can mean "complete or mature" (see 1 Cor. 14:20; Eph. 4:13; Heb. 5:14). See John D. Carter, "Maturity: Psychological and Biblical," *Journal of Psychology and Theology*, vol. 2 (Spring 1974), pp. 89-96.

3. *Macmillan Bible Atlas*, p. 93.

4. J. Cunningham Geikie, in *Hours with the Bible*, believes that Saul, following the slaughter of the priests, attacked the Gibeonites (see Sam. 22:18, 19). "Seized with remorse at his act, the unfortunate king appears to have determined in his blind way to atone to Jehovah for the outrage by showing his zeal against the heathen remnant of the native inhabitants" (III:162, 163). If this is true then it only illustrates the extremes of unreasoning legalism to which Saul would go to placate God for his violent outbursts of anger.

5. When the word *Arabah* is used with the article (as is most frequent), it refers to the wasteland area surrounding the Great Rift Valley. This valley runs south from the Sea of Galilee down the Jordan Valley and the Dead Sea area, and extends all the way to the Gulf of Akabah. (See *Unger's Bible Dictionary*, p. 75.)

6. Euphemistically described as "covering his feet" (see Judg. 3:24).

7. The supposed *word of the Lord* found in 1 Samuel 24:4 is difficult to interpret. Some writers imagine that it comes from 1 Samuel 15:28; 16:1,12; 20:15; and 23:17. Inasmuch as Saul fell by his own hand in a war with the Philistines, this "prophecy" cannot be of divine origin. It seems more likely that some pious individual gave utterance to it and that it was commonly believed by David's men. David certainly did not believe in it (see 1 Sam. 26:10).

8. The meaning of the Hebrew is generally rendered "waste" or "desert." The usage of the article limits its meaning to a specific area (e.g., Num. 21:20; 23:28; 1 Sam. 23; 19; 24). The term is used figuratively by the prophets to describe a nation left desolate by her enemies (Jer. 22:6; Hos. 2:3-5).

13
IT'S WINNING THAT COUNTS

1 SAMUEL 27:1—31:13

As the Lord Jesus finished His famous Sermon on the Mount, He told those who were listening to Him one of His memorable parables. He contrasted two men—the one wise and the other foolish—and used the house each one built to illustrate their respective destinies (Matt. 7:24-27). The key to the parable is found in Christ's words, *Everyone, therefore, who hears these words of mine and does them shall be like the prudent man who built his house upon the rock* (Matt. 7:26). We all have a choice; we can choose our destiny. What happens to us is vitally related to *how* we respond to the pressures that face us.

In no single passage of Scripture could the contrast of two destinies be more clearly defined than in the experiences of Saul and David. Both men made a choice earlier in their lives; both experienced God's involvement in their affairs (though in different ways); and both failed. David, however, repented of his departure from the Lord and was

restored to His favor, while Saul slipped ever deeper into
the quagmire of his sinful self-will.

David Fails to Trust God
1 Samuel 27:1-12; 28:1,2

When David and Saul part company at Engedi, we would
expect that from this time onward David's fortunes would
improve. He faced severe testings and showed, time and
again, the unalloyed gold of his character. Those who have
studied the strange psychology of the spirit know that there
are ebbs and flows in our experience. The strong current
which sweeps us to the heights of victory also has its rip-
tide. David's faith never glowed brighter than when he
restrained his men from killing Saul; but when Saul was
gone and he realized how the king had nearly taken him
and his men by surprise, and that now their last hiding
place had been uncovered, he gave way to faithless despair.
I shall now perish one day by the hand of Saul, he said;
*There is nothing better for me than to escape into the land
of the Philistines* (1 Sam. 27:1).

And so it is that David and his men,[1] their wives and
their families, and all they have, make their way to Achish,
king of Gath.

David does not enter Gath this time as a solitary fugitive,
but as an avowed enemy of Saul[2] and as the leader of a band
of well-trained men. He is warmly received by Achish and,
when the large influx of foreigners into the city poses an
embarrassment to the Philistine king, David is given the
village of Ziklag to live in (27:6; see Josh. 15:31; 19:5).
From this location he and his men make predatory raids
against the south country (27:8,9), and David takes care
that Achish receives his share of the spoils.[3] When the king
questions him about his activities, David deceives him into
believing that his attacks have been against Judah and her
allies (27:10-12); and Achish is taken in by his deceit.

During the 16 months David lives in Ziklag, the size of

his band increases (see 1 Chron. 12). While he is occupied in the Negev, the Philistines are busy preparing for war with Israel. When the armies of the city-states are summoned to a meeting, David is called upon to join forces with Achish. He has no alternative but to obey and he and his men journey north to Aphek.

David has never before lifted his hand against his own people and now he finds himself soon to be engaged in war with them. This must have caused him acute anguish of heart and it may well be that on the long march north he earnestly interceded with the Lord to extricate him from this predicament.

Saul Has No Place to Hide
1 Samuel 28:3-25

As all this is taking place, Saul and the army of Israel are making their camp at Gilboa. As Saul watches the Philistine armies increase in number, he becomes filled with fear and his heart utterly fails him. With no inner resources to strengthen him and no vital faith in God to undergird him during this hour of trial, he cries in desperation to the Lord, but *the LORD does not answer him, either by dreams or by Urim or by prophets* (28:6).

Sensing that the judgment pronounced by Samuel many years before is about to become a reality, Saul desires again to speak to the prophet. But Samuel has died and Saul has expelled all clairvoyants, necromancers, and spiritists from the land (28:3; see Lev. 20:27).[5] How then can he communicate with the prophet? He decides to seek out a woman possessed with an *Ob*, or demonic spirit, and ask her to bring Samuel before him.

At night, going behind enemy lines, Saul meets with the witch of Endor (28:8-14). She goes into a trance and at the request of Saul summons Samuel. She really expects her familiar spirit to come and impersonate the prophet and is totally unprepared when the real Samuel appears.[6] This so startles her that she let out a shriek. Saul reassures her[7] and then speaks to Samuel. *I am greatly distressed. The Philistines are waging war against me, and God [Elohim] has departed from me ... therefore, I have called for you, that you may make known to me what I shall do* (28:15).

Samuel's response clearly confirms what Saul already fears. *The LORD [Yahweh] has done to you as He spoke through me. He has torn the kingdom out of your hand and given it to your neighbor, even to David. As you did not obey the LORD and did not execute His fierce wrath on Amalek, so the LORD has done this thing to you this day* (28:17,18).

During Saul's entire reign—a period of time estimated by Bible scholars at between 33 and 40 years—he lived in disregard of the Word of God. He had ignored Samuel, the prophet of God, and persecuted David, the anointed of the Lord. Now his lifetime of self-will is being called into account. His sins have overtaken him. Tomorrow he will be in the place of the departed dead.[8] He has no place to hide.

Deliverance and Punishment
1 Samuel 29:1-11; 30:1-6

How different with David. As he and his men take their place among the Philistine battalions, the warlords see him and take exception to his presence. They voice their misgivings to Achish who, in turn, relays their feelings to David. While David is probably inwardly relieved he is very diplomatic in his response. To agree too quickly with the Gittite king might raise questions concerning his loyalty to the Philistine cause. Nevertheless, in obedience to Achish's wishes, he and his men spend the night in the Philistine camp, and early in the morning—the morning of the battle —they leave for Ziklag.

It takes David and his men two full days and a part of a third to reach their homes. When they arrive, footsore and weary, no children run out to meet them and none of their wives are there to set before them a warm meal.

Instead, only the charred remains of their homes meet their gaze, and the only things that stir are the ashes swirled about by the wind.

Few can imagine their bitter disappointment, and fewer still can sense the awful anguish each man felt as he wondered what happened to his wives and little ones.

The Amalekites had indeed taken revenge on David for his repeated raids on them (27:8). In the absence of adequate defenders, the town became an easy prey. After laying it waste, they took with them everything of value. The women and children were undoubtedly destined for Egypt where they would be sold on the slave market.

As the reality of what has happened pervades the conscious thinking of some of the men, acute anxiety and frustration wells up within them. They seek a scapegoat. Who caused them to leave their homes and go on an abortive march? And who left the city undefended? Some of the men who had apparently followed David with reluctance now speak out against him and institute a move to stone him. It is a dark day for David and he is distressed in spirit. In contrast to Saul, who grew increasingly afraid as the Philistine camp grew in size, David *strengthens his hand in his God* (30:6). He has resources to draw on which Saul knew nothing about.

The situation David faces at Ziklag is not new. Moses experienced a similar circumstance after leading the Israelites out of Egypt (see Exod. 17:4). And leaders of every age have found that rough, externally-oriented men are quick to react. While elated by success, they are just as easily depressed when the winds of adversity blow across their path; and they are quick to lash out against those whom they imagine to be at fault.

Back in God's Will
1 Samuel 30:7-31; 31:1-13

It often takes a crisis to bring us back to the Lord, and

this is the second one David has faced in recent days. He does not wait for God to speak to him through the lower forms of communication, such as dreams, but taking the initiative he calls for Abiathar the priest. *Bring me, I pray you, the ephod.* He then inquires of the Lord, *Shall I pursue the band? Shall I overtake them?* And the Lord answers, *Pursue, for you shall surely overtake them, and you shall surely rescue all* (30:7,8).

Being assured of God's blessing, David is able to encourage his men. He knows, from his long years as their leader, that externally-oriented men must be kept busy. He and his troop pursue the Amalekites and, in the special providence of God, find an Egyptian slave who is willing to serve as their guide.

David and his men soon overtake the Amalekites who, imagining themselves to be too far from Ziklag for any reprisal, are engaged in a careless and uproarious celebration for their success. David and his men stage a surprise attack. Every person and all the valuables the Amalekites looted are recovered. None among the women and children have been harmed.

This happy turn of events is celebrated by David in two separate ways. In the first place, *all* his men share equally in the spoils (30:9,10,21-25). And second, from what remains, David sends gifts to the elders of the cities in Judah. These he says are *a gift for you from the spoil of the enemies of the LORD* (30:26).

This latter act is as judicious as it is an expression of his recognition of God's favor. Undoubtedly David is desirous of making as favorable an impression on these leaders as possible. To be sure the Lord promised him the throne of Israel, but 16 months in another land may have dulled the minds of the people or caused them to doubt his loyalty. These gifts will be well received and remind the people of Judah of his former service.

While David has no means of knowing how the battle has

gone, he has been uprooted from his settled condition at Ziklag. In God's sovereignty the destruction of David's home—which outwardly might have been regarded as a calamity—has prepared him for the next phase of his service. In the course of time he will hear of the death of Saul and his sons and will mourn for them (see 2 Sam. 1:17-27). He will also ask the Lord for direction and be instructed to settle in Hebron. This will pave the way for the men of Judah to invite him to become their leader (see 2 Sam. 2:1-4). And so in David's experience, God's plan will be worked out in his life. All the details will be taken care of. And God's promise of long ago will be fulfilled.

In the Looking Glass

As we review the contents of 1 Samuel and refresh our minds of the difference between being internally or externally oriented, we need to remind ourselves that to be conditioned by external stimuli is part and parcel of the nature of man (see Rom. 8:5). And while many of us are content to live our lives this way, the path we tread is a dangerous one. Responding solely to outward experiences limits our world of reality. As the apostle Paul pointed out, living on the level of our lower natures and allowing our outlook to be formed by what we conceive of as being real, spells death (see Rom. 8:6). On the other hand, those who live on a spiritual level have a spiritual outlook, and this leads to life and peace.

Saul's experiences were externally conditioned. He was constantly threatened by fear. While the fear-objects took different forms, they were nevertheless persistent and so affected his mental and emotional health that, ultimately, his mind became unsettled. His was an anxiety without hope. David, on the other hand, willingly submitted himself to God's sovereignty. While he, too, failed on occasion and experienced inward distress, he was constantly being strengthened *in the inner man* (see Eph. 3:16). As a result

155

he could face adversity without losing his emotional equilibrium.

Because of his persistent disobedience and self-will, Saul saw God solely as an angry Parent who was constantly punishing him for what he did wrong. David also sinned and was chastened by the Lord, but his relationship with God was such that he responded to Him as a son with a loving Father.

In the final analysis, each man chose his own destiny. Throughout his life Saul abused what God gave him and, in the end, with nowhere to turn, he destroyed himself (see Hos. 13:11).[9] But David, after many trials and misfortunes, was ready emotionally and experientially to become Israel's king (see 1 Kings 2:33; 3:6; 8:16,66). The Spirit of God had so worked in his life that he could walk uprightly and do all God commanded him (see 1 Kings 9:4). And such was his influence over Israel that later generations referred to the Lord as *the God of David* (see 2 Kings 20:5; 2 Chron. 21:12). Furthermore, God continued to bless David's successors long after his death (see 2 Chron. 7:18), and his life and character became the "yardstick" by which other kings were judged (see 1 Kings 15:3,11; 2 Kings 14:3; 16:2; 18:3; 22:2; 1 Chron. 17:1,2; 2 Chron. 7:17,18; 28:1; 29:2; 34:2).

But how does all of this apply to us? How may we avoid the pitfalls into which Saul fell and follow the example of David (see Rom. 15:4; 1 Cor. 10:11)?

The answer is a relatively simple one.

In his book, *The Heart of Man*, Erich Fromm illustrates the reason for our failure. "A white boy of eight has a little friend, the son of a colored maid. Mother does not like him to play with the little negro, and tells her son to stop seeing him. The child refuses; mother promises to take him to the circus if he will obey; he gives in. This step of self-betrayal and acceptance of a bribe has done something to the little boy. He feels ashamed, his sense of integrity has been in-

156

jured, he has lost self-confidence. Yet nothing irreparable has happened. Ten years later he falls in love with a girl; it is more than an infatuation; both feel a deep human bond which unites them; but the girl is from a lower class than the boy's family. His parents resent the engagement and try to dissuade him; when he remains adamant they promise him a six months' trip to Europe if he will only wait to formalize the engagement until his return; he accepts the offer. Consciously he believes that the trip will do him a lot of good—and, of course, that he will not love his girl less when he returns. But it does not turn out this way. He sees many other girls, he is very popular, his vanity is satisfied, and eventually his love and his decision to marry become weaker and weaker. Before his return he writes her a letter in which he breaks off the engagement.

"When was the decision made? Not, as he thinks, on the day he writes the final letter, but on the day he accepted his parents' offer to go to Europe. He sensed, although not consciously, that by accepting the bribe he had sold himself —and he was to deliver what he promised: the break. His behavior in Europe was not the *reason* for the break, but the mechanism through which he succeeds in fulfilling the promise. At this point he has betrayed himself again, and the effects are increased self-contempt and (hidden behind the satisfaction of new conquests, etc.) inner weakness and lack of self-confidence. Need we follow his life any longer in detail? He ends up in his father's business, instead of studying physics, for which he has a gift; he marries the daughter of rich friends of his parents; he becomes a successful business and political leader who makes fatal decisions against the voice of his own conscience because he is afraid of bucking public opinion. His history is one of a hardening of the heart. One moral defeat makes him more prone to suffer another defeat, until the point of no return is reached. At eight he could have taken a stand and refused to take the bribe; he was still free. And maybe a friend, a grandfather, a teacher, hearing of his dilemma, might have helped him. At eighteen he was already less free; his future life was in the process of decreasing freedom, until the point where he lost the game of life."[10]

It was the same with Saul. He accepted the bribe (the things which pandered to his carnal appetites) and continued to accept the temporal over the spiritual until all thought of God and his responsibility to Him was lost. His life became filled with disillusionment and vain attempts to try and preserve the *status quo*. In the end he reaped exactly what he had sown. His death was the result of his self-will.

How different was David! He was a man of principle. He was shrewd and diplomatic, but free of those compromises which drown others in a sea of regret. Early in his life he submitted himself to the authority of the God of the covenant. His spiritual experience was real. He endured many trials and finally came to the place in his life where he could begin to enjoy all the things God promised him. In his experience there was no shame, no loss of integrity, no loss of confidence. The adversities he faced contributed to the maturing of his personality. He was, in every respect, a winner, a *man after God's own heart* (1 Sam. 13:14).

Interaction

1. From Christ's parable in Matthew 7:24-27 contrast the lives and destinies of Saul and David.

2. By failing to trust God and seeking refuge in Gath, David was unwittingly drawn into a compromising situation 16 months later. How could this have been avoided? What may we learn from his experience?

3. Externally-oriented people—men as well as women—must constantly be doing something. Why? How did David handle people such as this? What value is there in this method of operation?

4. Why had God spoken out against all forms of witchcraft? By

using a concordance and/or a Bible dictionary, make a list of the different manifestations of spiritism. Why are so many preoccupied with the occult today? In what ways is this a reflection of their external (rather than internal) orientation?

5. We all pass through experiences in which we feel we are being shaken loose from things which might tie us down. How do externally-oriented people respond to such events in their lives? How did David react? What may we learn from his experience that will be of help to us?

Footnotes

1. David's men now number 600. Their numbers have been increased by Israelites—many of them from Benjamin, Saul's tribe—who have grown dissatisfied with the king's rule (see 1 Chron. 12).

2. This, by popular report.

3. Alfred Edersheim, *Bible History*, vol. 4, p. 137. David's mode of life while at Ziklag was similar to Jephthah's (see Judg. 11). "This kind of military robbery was far from being considered dishonorable in the East. On the contrary, the fame acquired by these leaders was thought as fair as any that could be obtained through any class of military operation," *God Has the Answer* ... (pp. 135-40).

4. The sequence of inquiry mentioned in this verse shows its progressive stages—first dreams, then Urim, and finally prophets. Saul began his inquiry with the lowest form of ascertaining the divine will, and gradually ascended the scale. This passage must be reconciled with 1 Chron. 10:14. There it is stated that Saul did *not* inquire of the Lord. The solution seems to lie in the fact that Saul did not really seek the Lord in the sense of wanting direction and of being willing to be guided by the information he received. All he wanted to know was the outcome of the battle and its effect on him. With such an attitude it is no wonder the Lord did not communicate with him.

5. After Samuel's death, Saul wished to give the people an example of his own religious zeal. His expulsion of all spiritists, witches, and warlocks from the land, while right (see Lev. 19:31; Deut. 18:10-14; Isa. 8:19; 19:3), was in reality another example of his legalism.

6. This view of what is recorded is espoused by Merrill F. Unger, *Biblical Demonology* (Wheaton: Scripture Press, 1952), pp. 148-152; Edersheim, *Bible History*, vol. 4, pp. 141,142; and J.J. Davis, *The Birth of a Kingdom*, pp. 97-100.

7. Saul, who never submitted to the provisions of God's covenant with Israel, and who had been forsaken by the Lord *(Yahweh)*, did not hesitate to use His name when making oath (1 Sam. 28:10). This type of an oath,

considering his business with the witch, shows his complete lack of spiritual sensitivity.

8. Evidence of Saul's unspiritual condition may be seen from the fact that he showed no signs of repentance, no softening of heart at the prediction of his ruin. In stolid desperation he went to meet his doom. But what of Samuel's words in 28:19? In *Biblical Demonology* (pp. 151, 152), Dr. Unger enlarges upon the "two compartments" of the underworld. The place of the righteous dead was called "Paradise" and was emptied when the Lord Jesus arose from the dead (see Luke 23:43; see also Luke 16:18-31; note vv. 22-26). The other part of the underworld was a place of torment. Now, since Christ's resurrection, believers who die go immediately into His presence. Saul did not go to the place of the righteous dead, but to the section where the unrighteous dead are being kept pending the day of judgment. Samuel's words to Saul in 28:19 are similar to the words of Dives in Luke 16:18-31.

9. During the battle Saul is wounded by the archers. His great fear is that the Philistines will take him alive and abuse him (see Judg. 16:23-31). In desperation he asks his armor bearer to kill him. His armor bearer refuses. Saul then falls on his own sword and, as far as any eyewitness is concerned, he "dies." In 2 Samuel we read that an Amalekite (see 1 Sam. 15:1-3) comes across Saul. Saul perhaps recovered consciousness and, seeing the Amalekite, asked him to end his life. Acting on Saul's request, he kills him (see 2 Sam. 1:5-10). This interpretation fits in with Samuel's statement that Saul would be slain (not kill himself).

10. Erich Fromm, *The Heart of Man* (New York: Harper & Row, 1964), pp. 137,138.

160